EL DORADO FREDDY'S

Chain Restaurants in Poems and Photographs

EL DORADO FREDDY'S

Chain Restaurants in Poems and Photographs

poems: Danny Caine
photographs: Tara Wray

Belt Publishing

Printed in the United States of America
First edition 2020

ISBN: 978-1-948742-62-7

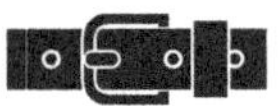

Belt Publishing
3143 W 33rd Street #6
Cleveland Ohio 44109
www.beltpublishing.com

Book design by Meredith Pangrace
Cover by David Wilson

Dedications:

Danny:

for Jack

Tara

for Bessie Wray, 1926-2017

"So I decided it would work if I went to every restaurant in town. That would mean places such as Taco John's, McDonald's, and the truck stops. To me, these places are interesting. And plenty of people eat in them."

—Marilyn Hagerty, *Grand Forks*

"The hamburger is distinctly popular only in states west of the Mississippi River and east of the Rocky Mountains."

—A Wichita newspaper in 1925, quoted in David Gerard Hogan's *Selling 'em By the Sack: White Castle and the Creation of American Food*

"We spend our entire lives assuming that buildings are permanent, and that, on this basis, we can revisit our pasts."

—Kate Wagner, "The Archivists of Extinction"

CONTENTS

PROLOGUE

El Dorado Freddy's began on Twitter. Absently scrolling one day, I came across a thread promising to rank "all the chain restaurants' chicken nuggets." The representative sampling was, suffice to say, nowhere near "all" the possible nuggets. The thread was neither complete nor insightful, and I was certain I could do better.

Later, I found myself on the way to an evening work assignment needing a quick dinner. I was on the south end of town, where all the chain restaurants are, so I pulled into a Popeye's. The resulting delicious meal reminded me of the nuggets tweet, and my experience at Popeyes was weird and poignant enough that I wrote a poem about it. The poem ended up reviewing the restaurant as well, and I liked the idea of a poem that works as a poem and also as a restaurant review.

Later, again on Twitter, Aaron Burch posted a call for weird column ideas for his journal *Hobart*, which had published me a few times before. I sent him a proposal for a series of restaurant review poems, and he loved it. We eventually ran eight of these, once a month. When the first poem ran, I got an email through the contact form on my website from Tara Wray asking, in part, "Would you be interested in taking a few days this summer and hitting as many chains as possible with me? I would take pictures and you do the writing and we could self-publish it in book form." Fortunately, Belt Publishing was kind enough to offer us a contract so we won't have to self-publish it. Aside from that, things happened exactly as Tara proposed.

I had seen Tara's work before. I love her brilliant image of a cat eating squirt cheese, as well as the one depicting a donut tragically crushed beneath the top of its cake stand. Her sensitive exploration of living with depression, as well as her eye for landscape and her dark sense of humor, were a perfect fit. I instantly loved the idea of collaborating.

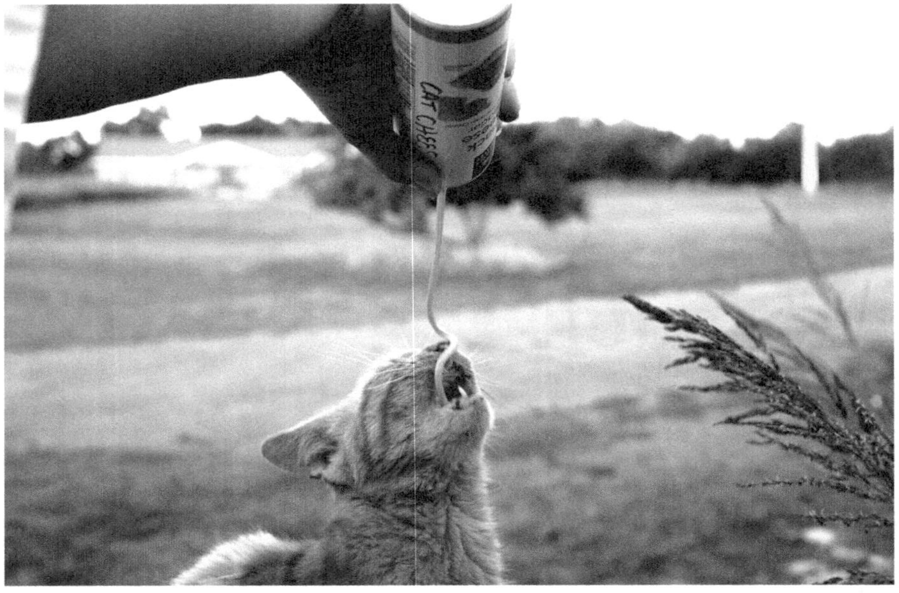

The commercial landscape that interests us is equal parts linguistic and visual, full of hyperbolic slogans, optimistic menus, neon lights, and saturated colors. Any meditation on what it means to be a chain restaurant consumer must be based in both language and image.

What follows is a visual and poetic consideration of nostalgia, chicken fingers, parenting, identity, and politics in a Midwestern landscape where people often eat at chain restaurants, even when they have "better" choices available. Even though these kinds of places don't often show up in poems. Think of this as two small books bound together, one with a portfolio of poems and one with a portfolio of photographs. In the dialogue between them, we hope a portrait of this neglected yet ubiquitous landscape emerges.

—Danny Caine and Tara Wray, February 2019

CHICKEN NUGGET

The chicken nugget was invented in the 1950s by Robert C. Baker, a food scientist at Cornell University *see also* out of frustration with my childhood picky eating, my mother once asked me to write down all the foods I actually would eat *see also* McDonald's added chicken nuggets to their menu in 1980 after buying the recipe from Tyson in 1979 *see also* one of the items on my list was Thanksgiving dinner, two others were Burger King and Wendy's chicken nuggets, but not McDonald's *see also* the town of Tonganoxie, Kansas successfully rallied grassroots support to sink a plan to build a Tyson processing plant there *see also* there is no McDonald's in Tonganoxie *see also* in January 2019 Tyson announced the recall of 36,420 pounds of chicken nuggets because customers were finding rubber in them *see also* the concept of the chain restaurant originated in Kansas, with Fred Harvey's Harvey Houses along the Santa Fe Railroad *see also* Wendy's nuggets still taste and look the same, but somewhere along the line Burger King changed its recipe *see also* the first fast food chain, White Castle, was founded in Wichita, Kansas in 1921 *see also* During early 2019's record-length government shutdown the national champion Clemson Tigers football team visited the White House where Donald Trump had personally bought them 300 Wendy's and McDonald's hamburgers, plus at least some chicken nuggets, calling it all "great American food" *see also* the site of the first White Castle is an office building and there is no plaque or anything *see also* these places have nostalgia but not history *see also* the last White Castles in Kansas closed during (and because of) World War II's food and labor shortages *see also* the most retweeted tweet of 2017 was a teen named @carterwjm asking Wendy's how many retweets it would take for a year of free chicken nuggets *see also* it was retweeted 3.6 million times and it successfully earned young Carter free nuggets for a year

OLIVE GARDEN

Nights that felt unlimited like salad n' breadsticks:
mom's car, a cashed bag boy paycheck, another exit,
another country. Parking lot Italy, no passport needed,
just a flashing buzzer. This was all we knew of fancy.
We just couldn't swing that many dates where dinner
cost more than ten bucks each. I see them winking
when they discuss this place, even when they try
to be kind. *Okay, fine*, they say. *The salad is actually good.*
Of course the salad is good, it's America's national dish.
I don't have time for their winks because if I don't
leave now, the line will be too long when I get there.
Good thing the pasta, like the salad, like us, never ends.

Address: 15090 W. 119th St., Olathe, KS 66062
Eaten: Seafood Alfredo, Grilled Chicken Parmigana, Italian Margarita, Salad n' Breadsticks ($52)
With: Poet + Kara
Why: I have begun working on a book of poetry about chain restaurants. If this is going to be the bible of chain restaurant poetry, it must begin in the Garden.

WENDY'S

On the way to T's childhood Wendy's I tell her
about mine, a Fancy Wendy's, with a salad bar,
rooms, tin ceilings or something. I've been too afraid
to go back: no person ever steps into the same Wendy's
twice. T wants to take photos of hers but we arrive
to find a letter on the door. As of last December's fire,
the building is unsafe to occupy. A plastic tree still leans
against the window. They didn't even have time
to put the chairs up. This Wendy's is now open
only in T's memory and nothing has changed
since she came here with her grandparents years ago.
T smiles. Inside this Wendy's, they are still alive.
We can't go in, but it's enough to cloud this glass
with breathing, trying to get a picture.

Address: 3006 Anderson Ave., Manhattan, KS 66503
Eaten: n/a
With: Poet + T
Why: Nostalgia is a GPS

POPEYE'S LOUISIANA KITCHEN

The man at the microphone
tells me I'm guest number 138—
a guest, but a number nonetheless.
I guess I'm not in Panera anymore.
The chicken tenders taste
exactly like chicken tenders

and the green beans swim
in salty goop. A sign on the wall
says "over 300 years ago, seven
distinctive culinary traditions came
together to create THE uniquely American
cuisine." They must mean the chicken tender.

When it opened here, Popeye's needed
a rent-a-cop to direct drive-thru traffic
as visored employees clipboarded the line.
Tonight is calmer: quiet zydeco burbles
punctured by a manager who aced
the training session about shouting.

Something in the book I'm reading makes me
miss Aunt Pat. When she was alive, I was
picky. A strict chicken tendertarian. I wish
I could explain to her that I like fancy
restaurants now, like she did, that I'm sorry
I dragged her to so many Burger Kings

and Popeye's. And I do. But I'm still
called guest 138. These are the places
I actually went with her, not the places
I wish I could've. Aunt Pat had taste,
but what I thought was good
was good enough for her.

Address: 2560 Iowa St., Lawrence, KS 66046
Eaten: 5 piece spicy tenders meal with green beans and Diet Coke ($9-something)
With: Poet, alone
Why: Between errands and selling books at an offsite reading, a quiet moment to sit in the corner booth, watching the sun set behind the American Family Insurance, and read the end of Hanif Abdurraqib's *They Can't Kill Us Until They Kill Us*.

ON THE BORDER MEXICAN GRILL & CANTINA

Why the hell is it so hard to get every friend
into one restaurant at the same time? But
it's our only idea of how to tell people: no Facebook
bullshit, no baked goods shenanigans. Put everyone
at a table and tell them. That's as far as the plan got.
Lele loves this place's happy hour, so here we are
but Lele is in the process of flaking while we decide
whether to order or not. How about drinks: Kara
asks for water and I think Kate notices. The margaritas
take too long to get here and I'm dying, can't think
of anything to say. Anything else to say. They arrive.
I propose a toast. Everyone says "cheers" and I say
"we're pregnant!" The pause that follows
is better than any of the food here.

Address: On The Border Mexican Grill & Cantina, 3080 Iowa St., Lawrence, KS 66046: NOW CLOSED
Eaten: Taco Salad, Grilled Fish Tacos Del Mar, a big margarita (something like 30 bucks)
With: Poet + Kara + Kate + Hannah + Jacob + Megan. Lele did join up later. She got her own thing that involved *Jeopardy* and it's the only part we remembered to record on video.
Why: Everybody says not to tell anyone until 12 weeks, but nobody says how hard it is to wait that long.

IN-N-OUT BURGER

Animal style: mustard patty,
extra spread, griddled onions.

Baby style: all over the floor.

Toddler style: negotiating a cocoa
in exchange for three more bites
then storing the bites in-mouth
until the cocoa arrives, then spitting out
all the bites. *See also*: chipmunk style.

Martha style: some kind of experiment
in finding the perfect In-N-Out order
which ends up being lots of single veggies
in wax paper bags. She should give up—
the double-double animal style is
the LeBron James of fast food burgers—
the best ever, and not available in Ohio.

California Style: stop for potty later
at the Jelly Belly factory, where the pizzas
are jellybean-shaped and jellybeans can taste
like donuts and "Nasty Girl" plays
in the caseload room where fart beans
are on closeout. Then south to Oakland.
Watch the hills turn Windows XP green
and play Fleetwood Mac loud enough
to get the kids to sleep. Absorb it—
this is the extra spread to put
on the Culvers-at-best life which awaits
after leaving California and these kids again.

Nostalgia style: I miss my Double Double
before I even take a bite. I know babies
become toddlers, toddlers become kids,
friends become long distance friends,
burgers become slimy wax paper
crumbles: never break the chain.

Address: In-N-Out Burger: 130 Grass Valley Highway, Auburn, CA 95603
Eaten: 2 double-double animal styles plus another with tomato, pickle, and lettuce on the side for some reason, 1 plain cheeseburger, 3 small fries, extra spread, a hot cocoa which is free for kids on rainy days ($26.39)
With: Poet + Kara + Martha + Martha's baby + Martha's toddler
Why: When in Rome.

CULVER'S

We've never lived in Culver's territory and it still doesn't
feel like we do. I mean, it's like a 15-minute drive.

In Ohio we drove 15 minutes for groceries and 45
for work but here we only drive that long

if we have to. Tonight we have to
have custard and Kara has to have the baby

stop kicking her bladder for like ten minutes at least
and Culver's has to stop putting calorie counts

on their menu. Jesus. The custard is fine, the mint
tastes synthetic and the strawberry tastes like an alien

spent years studying the concept of "strawberry"
and longer trying to replicate it. For crying out loud

just get a Butterburger and curds. I hear
a cashier say *all our burgers are Butterburgers, so.*

Is that a Midwest thing? The trailing *so*?
My phone tells me that, actually

there *are* Culver's in Ohio. 10 of them,
with an 11th coming soon in Avon, so

a 15-minute drive from our old place. The northernmost
Waffle House is in Toledo. There are no regions left—

someday New Jersey will sprout In-N-Outs. Someday
we'll get double doubles at a Mississippi Tim Horton's.

Tonight we just hold hands into the year's first warm evening,
across a soft pretzel sidewalk that could be anywhere else.

Address: 2111 W 33rd St., Lawrence, KS 66046
Eaten: 1 mini concrete mixer with mint and Oreo, 1 scoop of flavor of the day (Double Strawberry) in a cone ($6.08)
With: Poet + Kara
Why: Valentine's Day, after dinner. The Salvation Army bummed us out but we weren't ready to go home.

MCDONALD'S

Online I see
a picture of nuggets.
A caption: "I'm in love
with the shape of you." How
many nugget shapes are there?
Two? or three? I'm in love with
her (pregnant) and me (had a few), in
the drive through line because we both
have a silly craving for nuggets but for
different reasons. Remember when sweet
and sour sauce was round like a belly? I
love her in any shape. Oh, we are going
to be parents. My parents sometimes
didn't want to cook, took us on a fast
food cruise of different drive-thrus
instead. Are we going to do this?
I don't want to, if only because
I don't want this—nuggets
in the dark, me drunk
and her rolling
her eyes—
to ever
end.

Address: McDonald's, 1309 W 6th St., Lawrence, KS 66044
Eaten: honestly, this happened quite a bit, but nuggets in six piece increments ($3.29) and a small M&M McFlurry ($1.89).
With: Poet + Kara
Why: This McDonald's is visible (and often audible) from our apartment. The person sitting in what will become the nursing chair can hear the drive-through warble. This McDonald's is a presence in our home, even if we can't at the moment smell the combination of nugget and paper bag.

CRACKER BARREL

It could be my last quiet night: I'm off work
at four, your mom is in class until nine. 37 weeks.
All day I look forward to hours of empty house
then I'm there and the whole place itches. I go
not home but the place that tries so hard to feel like it.
As always, the rifle hangs over the fireplace. As always
the bathroom is under the stoplight. A sign in there
says "do not leave baby unattended." Good advice
is everywhere these days. As always, the receipt printer
spits out my seat. As always I order the same thing
and it's the same delicious as always. No, earthquake—
I don't dread your arrival. I'm in awe of your power
to alter, to knock the world's rocking chairs out of line.
That you'll disarray even a place so perfectly same.

Address: 1421 SW Ashworth Pl., Topeka, KS 66604
Eaten: Chicken Tenderloins Dinner with honey mustard sauce. Sides: double green beans and turnip greens (with hot vinegar sauce). Yes biscuits. Grape jelly. Diet Coke (Something like 13 bucks)
With: Poet, alone
Why: Hanif has a new poem in *Poetry*, and the only place to buy it is the awful Barnes & Noble in Topeka, and while I'm there, might as well.

CHICKEN TENDER

A restaurant called The Puritan in Manchester, New Hampshire claims to have invented the Chicken Tender in 1974 *see also* I don't remember my first chicken tender *see also* When I was a child in the early 1990s, "healthy" meant low fat which led to a spike in production of chicken breasts which in turn led to a surplus of chicken breast by-products like the pectoralis minor muscle, commonly known as the tenderloin *see also* the chicken tenders from Arby's were always a spicier, more expensive alternative to chicken nuggets, good for a night when the suburban child is feeling adventurous *see also* the abundance of the tenderloin muscle as by-product led to the prominence of chicken tenders on children's menus in the 1990s *see also* the best chicken tenders were at our location of a chain called Rockne's, where I would order an adult portion of six and sub potato chips for the fries *see also* they were perfect with honey mustard and a sprinkling of salt *see also* to this day I'm dealing with hypertension, like many others in my family *see also* if one were to ask my parents, there were days when it was either chicken tenders or going to bed hungry.

TEXAS ROADHOUSE VOL. 1

We're waiting for our most important anecdote
to start. *Every place now could be the place*
you go into labor, I tell Kara. She says
you know you want it to be here.

The hostesses always walk so slow
to the table, always ask if we're celebrating
anything. We could be, I think. I almost
answered two point five when they asked

how many tonight. Our baby will be born
in America so it might as well be here,
where a person in an "I ♥ MY JOB" shirt
line dances right past the booth

while Kara's in the bathroom. *Did I miss*
dancing? Damn! The first Texas Roadhouse
was in Indiana. The food tastes like
this is Cracker Barrel's little brother

who drinks too much and sleeps too late.
Kara tells me she ate too much last time,
so I should hide the rolls. I do. The waitress
sees a breadless table and brings more.

We've had lots of last times but this is really it
for just-us nights: Her mom gets here
tomorrow, the due date is Sunday. Why
are we here and not anywhere else?

It's close to Target, Kara says, *and I've heard*
I'll really miss little things like going to the store
alone. Our list has two things on it but we still
spend a hundred and fifty-five dollars.

Address: 2329 Iowa St., Suite T, Lawrence, KS 66046
Eaten: Grilled BBQ chicken dinner with double green beans, a diet coke, a grilled shrimp appetizer, a side Caesar salad, a side of mac and cheese, and a water ($34.41)
With: Poet + Kara, future parents
Why: The baby needs a hamper, right? And we should get some snacks for the go-bag.

DOMINO'S PIZZA

They don't mention that the kitchen closes
at 7:00. If a baby is born at, say, 8:07,
all the new parents get is a shrugging nurse
saying *we've got juice boxes and Teddy Grahams.*
Plus I'm pretty sure Domino's can deliver up here.
They can't. An hour after I call (two hours?
15 minutes? Time gets fucked the minute
a first child is born) my phone buzzes.
The Domino's guy is stuck outside
the emergency room entrance with all
the late night full moon folks waiting
for the security guard to get back
from wherever he went. I take the pizza,
and wait for my turn with the guard.
I turn to the dude next to me and I say it
out loud for the first time: *I'm a dad.*
I take a slice of pizza. I haven't eaten
since breakfast. The dude says, *me too, man.*
I want to say the pizza was good. It wasn't.

Where: Domino's Pizza, 832 Iowa St., Lawrence, KS 66044
What: Large pizza with half pepperoni, half mushrooms & onions (I lost the receipt—it was maybe 20 bucks?)
Who: Poet in the parking lot, trying to get back to Kara & the Baby
Why: This town has a famous delivery pizza place—everyone who's lived here more than five years has their phone number jingle memorized. It's also famously cash only, and the ATM was on the to-do list for the day Kara went into labor. We didn't get to it. Hungry, exhausted, I settled for the pizza I could most easily order from my phone without using it as a phone.

TEXAS ROADHOUSE VOL. 2

These bluejeaned teens in shirts
that say "I ♥ MY JOB" always ask:
Are we celebrating anything tonight?
Yes: we're celebrating getting out
of the goddamn house showered
with passable outfits on.

Every book says I'll miss this part.
Maybe early fatherhood is a state
best imagined from elsewhere, like this
Texas: imagined in Indiana, deposited
before a fading Sears in Kansas.
I love it here. You can't appreciate

waiters dancing in the aisle, staring
above all our heads. But I can.
How they keep chicken breasts
this moist is probably something
I don't want to know. And holy moly
these green beans. I ask Kara for hers

but she says *that's an awful lot*
of sodium. I've already eaten two orders.
We've become parents. My parents
say they're proud, that we're doing
a good job. But there are days when
I'm line dancing because I have to.

Address: 2329 Iowa St., Suite T, Lawrence, KS 66046
Eaten: My parents and I both ordered some variation on the BBQ chicken dinner. Kara got the four-sides-as-an-entrée but skipped her usual mac and cheese because we're still not sure if the baby has a dairy insensitivity. I didn't get the total because my dad insisted on paying.
With: Poet + Kara + the Baby + the Poet's Parents
Why: When you find a place that everyone agrees on—poet, wife, son, grandma, grandpa—you go. You go often.

APPLEBEE'S

After James Wright

1.

Bob Evans and Fuddruckers both
had baby-impossible lines. Every table
at Applebee's is either empty or full
of other families trying to salvage
their Father's Day. Where be the jerseys
on the wall, the benevolent manager
staying open so the rainy football team
can eat after the hard loss? This is only
a neighborhood bar and grill if
the neighborhood is a hotel lobby
in 2003. I used to think margaritas
were like sex but this one proves me wrong.
Sometimes bad is just bad. They say millennials
are killing this place: maybe it's a good idea.
I'm not even sure what Bourbon Street
Shrimp n' Chicken *is* except bland
and brown. This neighborhood is
a nightmare of urban planning, all
frontage road and parking lot parking lots.
Take the wrong left and get disoriented
just like Applebee's. Kara can't figure out
how to feed you in the booth.
I pay on the stupid touchscreen thing.
There's a first time for everything: first child,
first time using the touchscreen thing.
We retreat from our last time
at Applebee's to a parking lot with a view
of another parking lot.

2.

This is only a neighborhood bar and grill
if the neighborhood is memories
of Friday nights after football games,
the smell of band uniform sweat
in the big corner booth. They tell me
the chicken tenders are infinite. They ask me
if I want more before I can take my first bite.

Where: 1. Applebee's, 1700 Village W. Pkwy., Kansas City, KS 66111
2. Applebee's, 2520 Iowa St., Lawrence, KS 66046

Eaten: 1. Margarita, Bourbon Street Shrimp & Chicken, Thai Shrimp Salad (I don't remember how much it cost because I couldn't figure out how to make the touchscreen thing print)
2. Grilled Shrimp Caesar Salad + Unlimited Chicken Tenders and a Diet Pepsi ($35.85)

Who: 1. Poet + Kara + the Baby
2. Poet + Kara + the Baby

Why: 1. I knew being a father would change me, but not to the extent that my first response when Kara asks what I want to do for my first Father's Day would be "let's go to the outlet mall to get some more onesies."
2. I see an ad in my Instagram feed for unlimited chicken tenders and it stays in my subconscious all day until we discuss what to do for dinner.

PHOTOGRAPHS

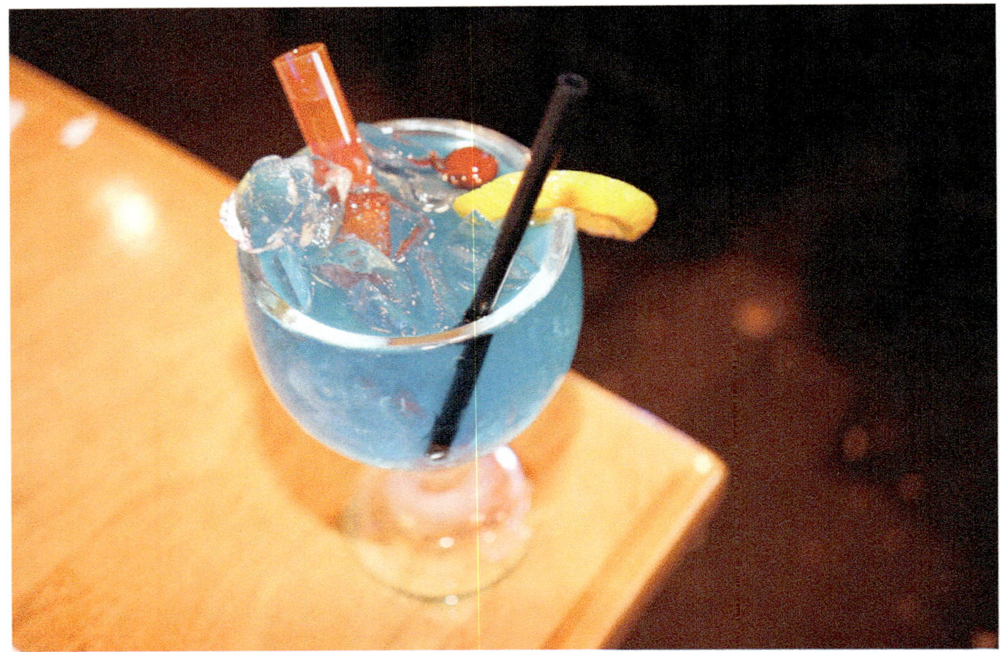

Blue Drink, Lawrence, KS, 2018

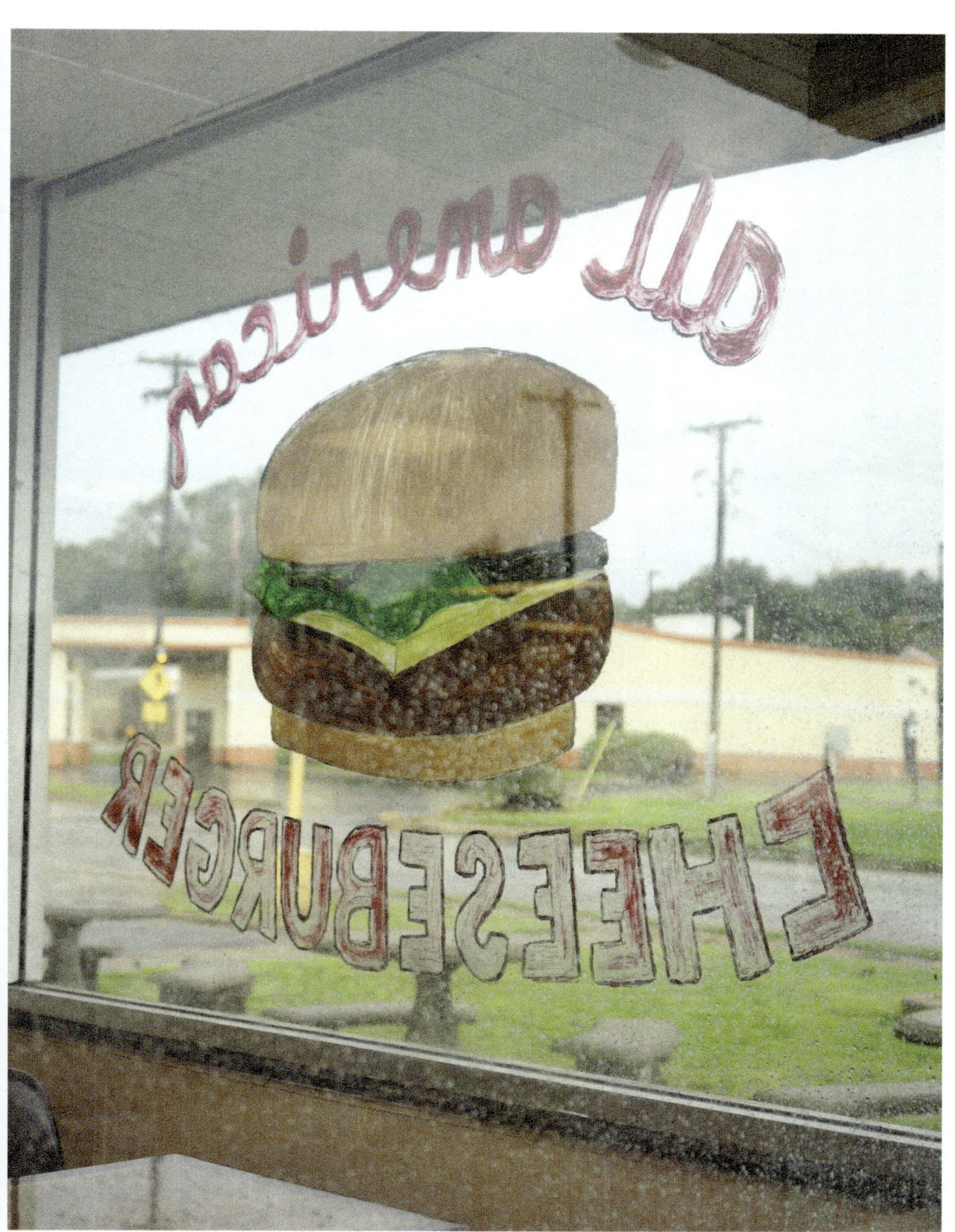

Cheeseburger Window, St. Joseph, MO, 2018

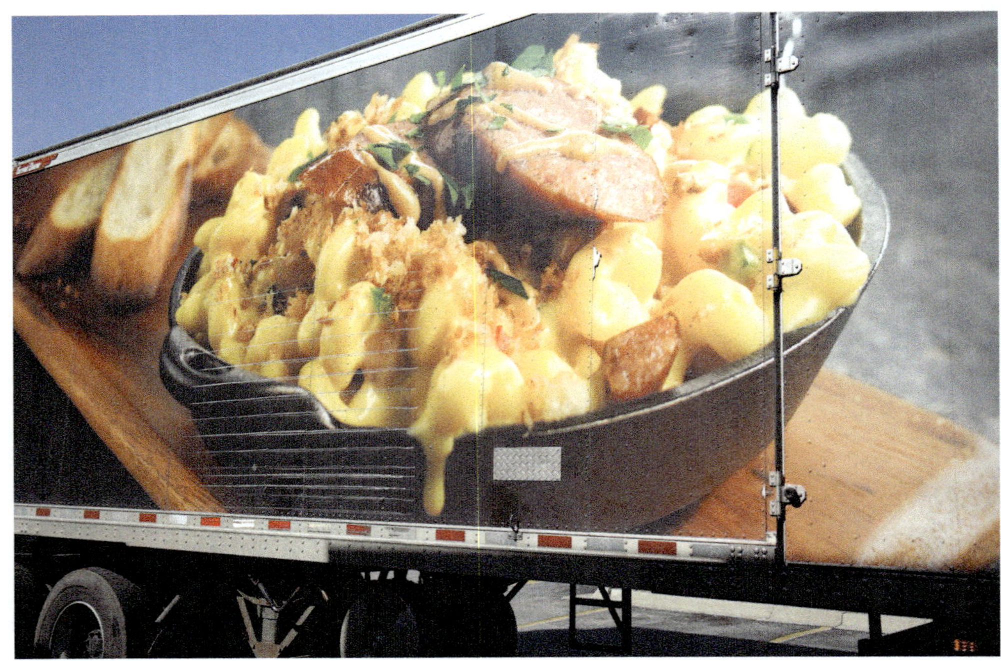

Cheesy Skillet Truck, Lawrence, KS, 2018

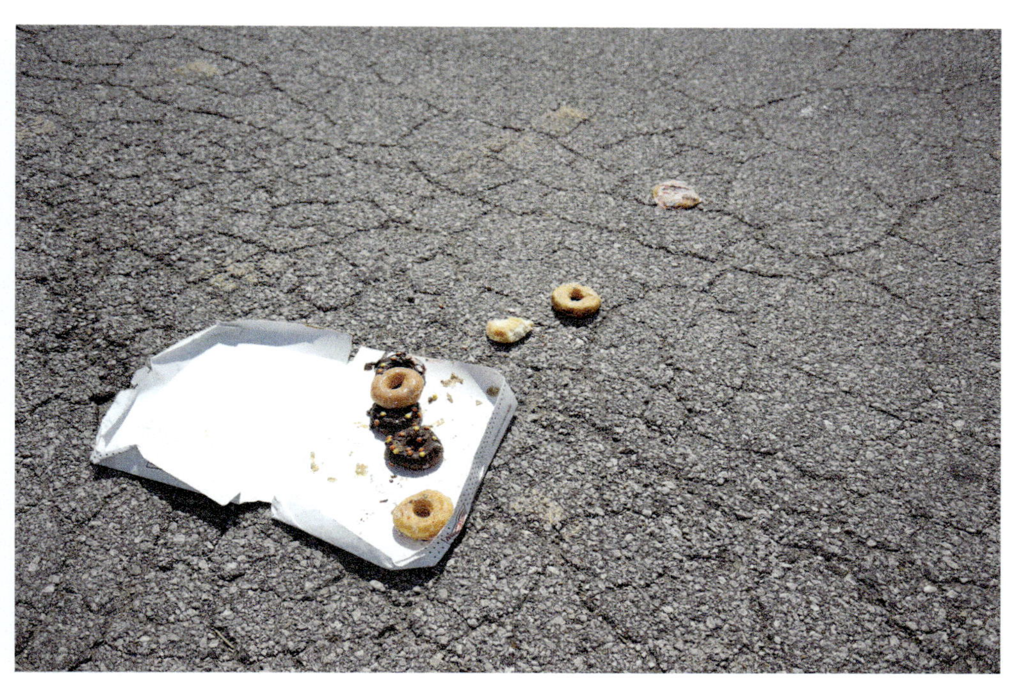

Donuts in a Parking Lot, Merriam, KS, 2018

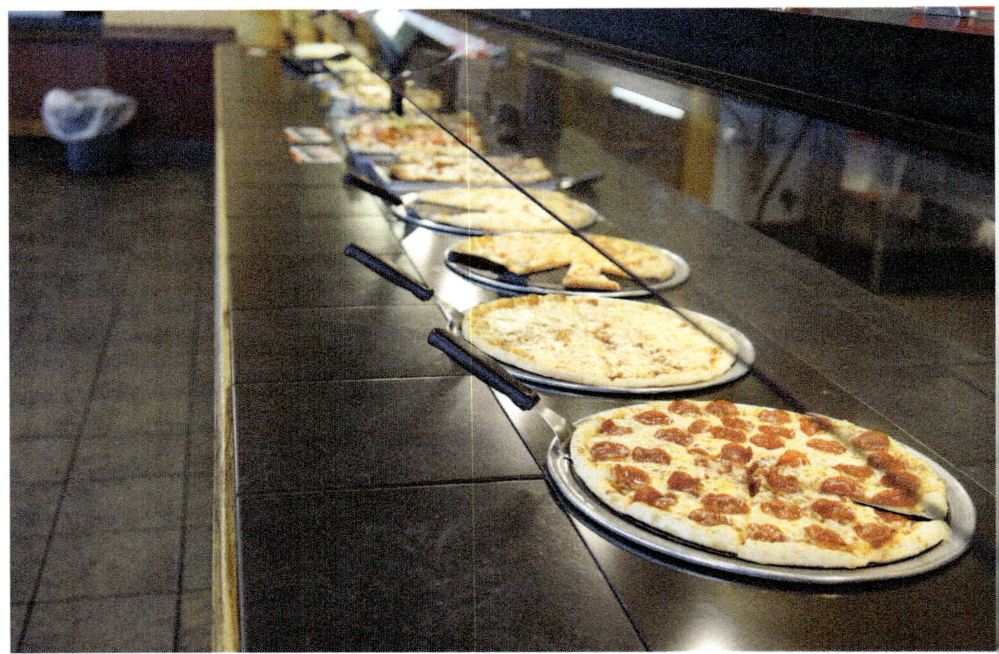

Pizza Row, Lawrence, KS, 2018

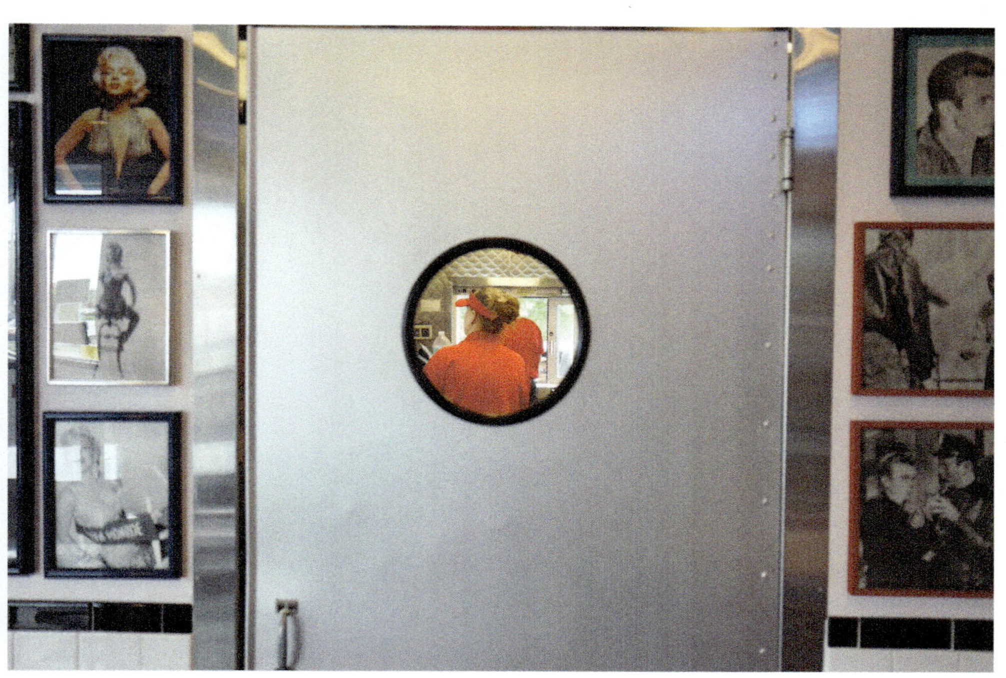

Peek Inside the Kitchen, Topeka, KS, 2018

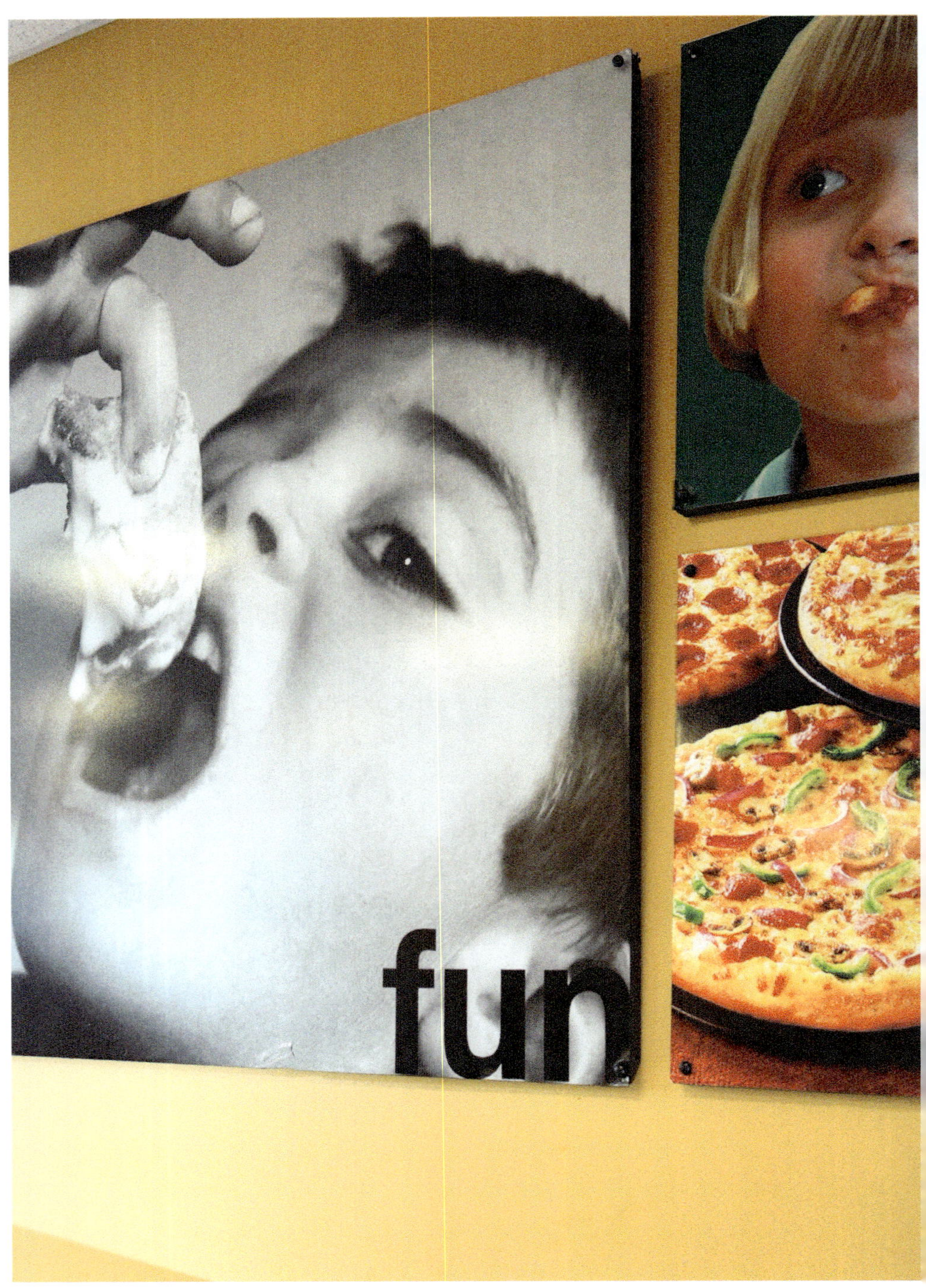

Fun, Lawrence, KS, 2018

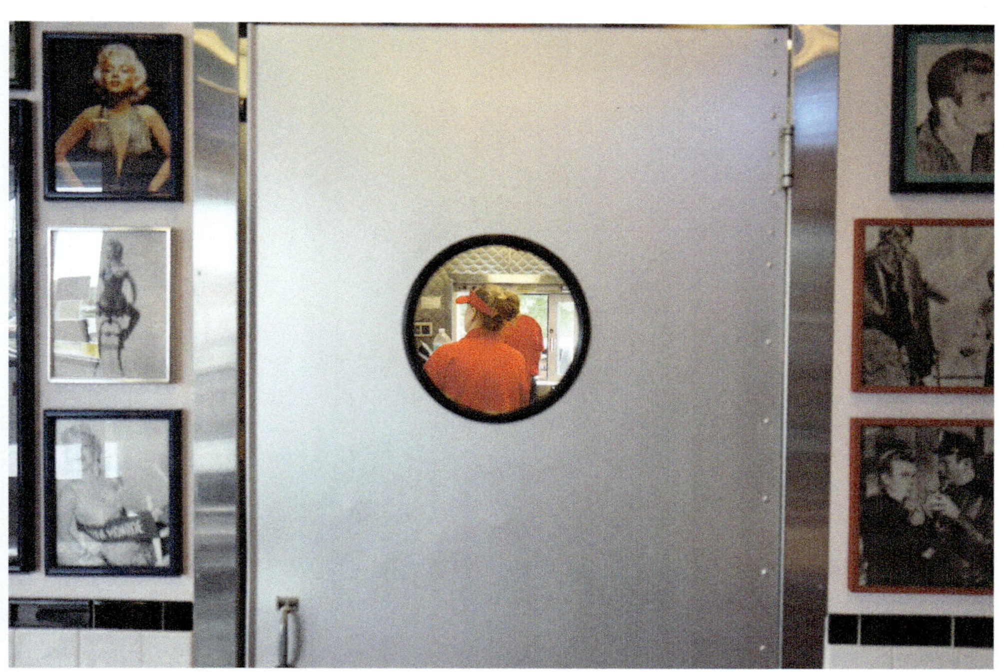
Peek Inside the Kitchen, Topeka, KS, 2018

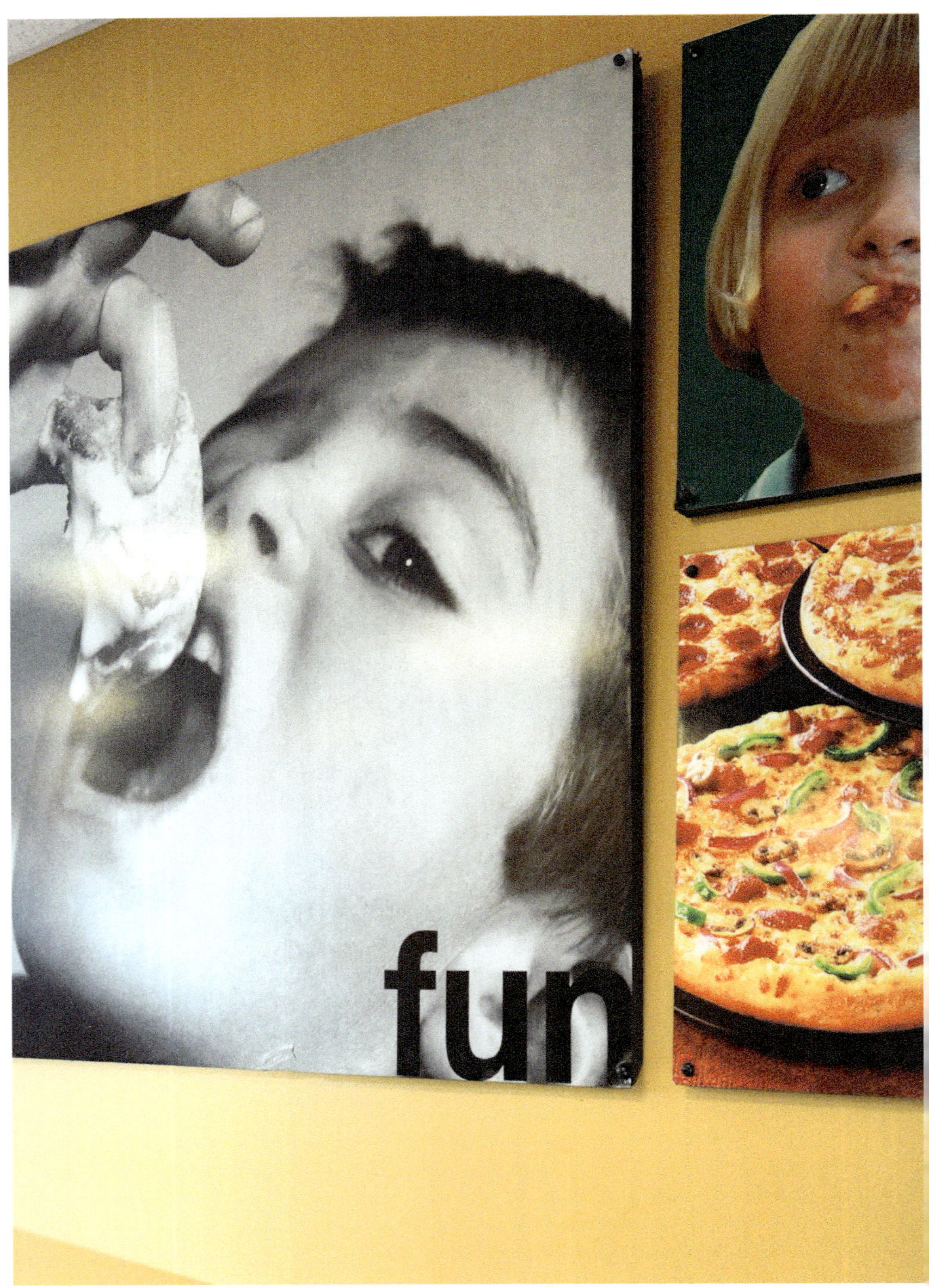

Fun, Lawrence, KS, 2018

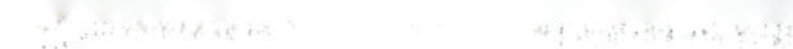

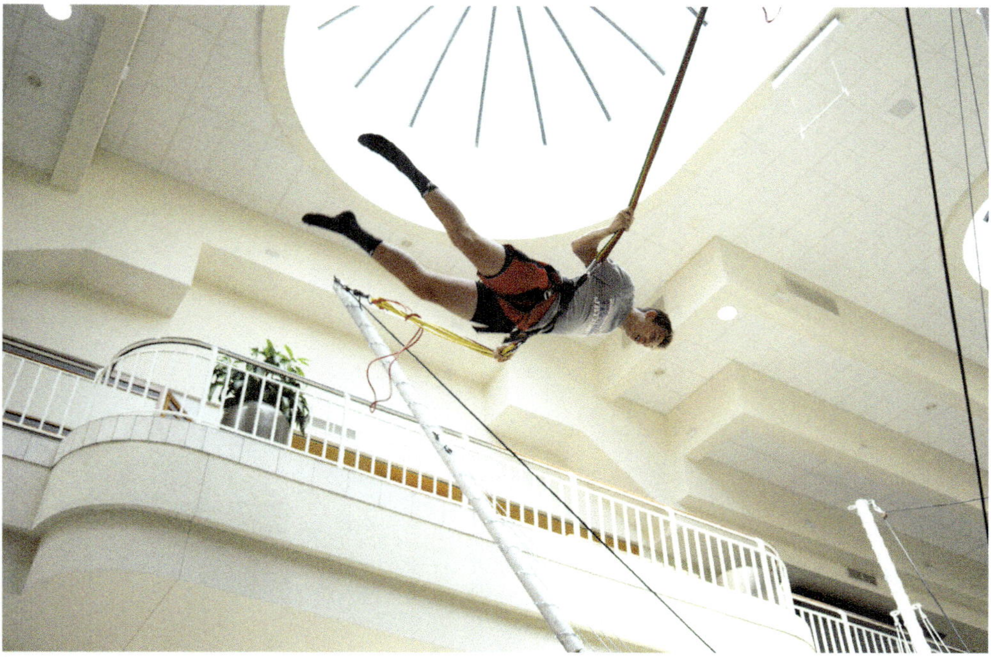

Mall Bungee, Topeka, KS, 2018

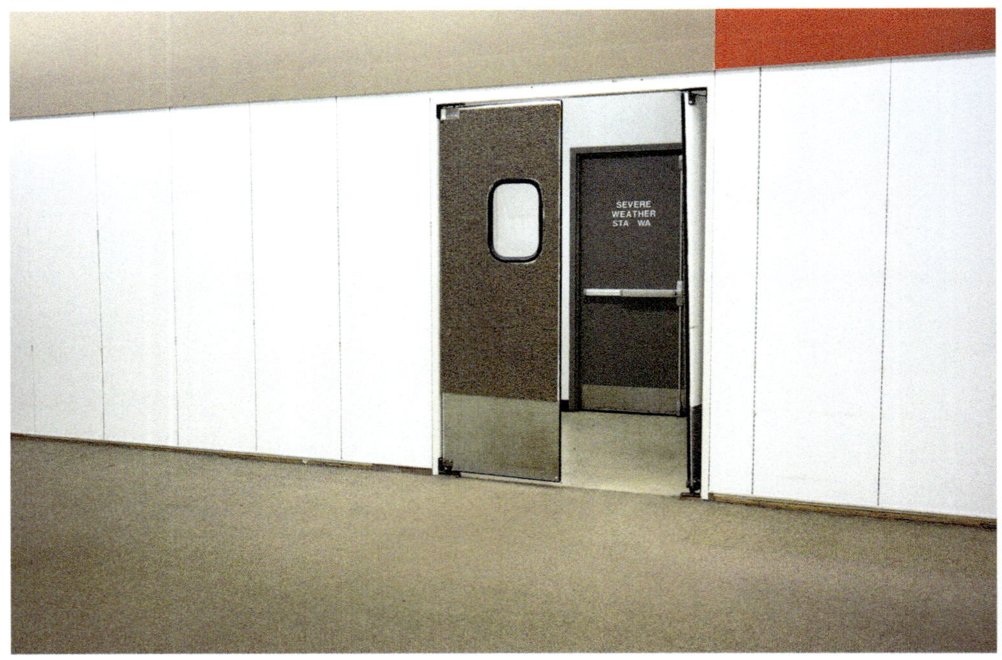

Mall Shelter, Topeka, KS, 2018

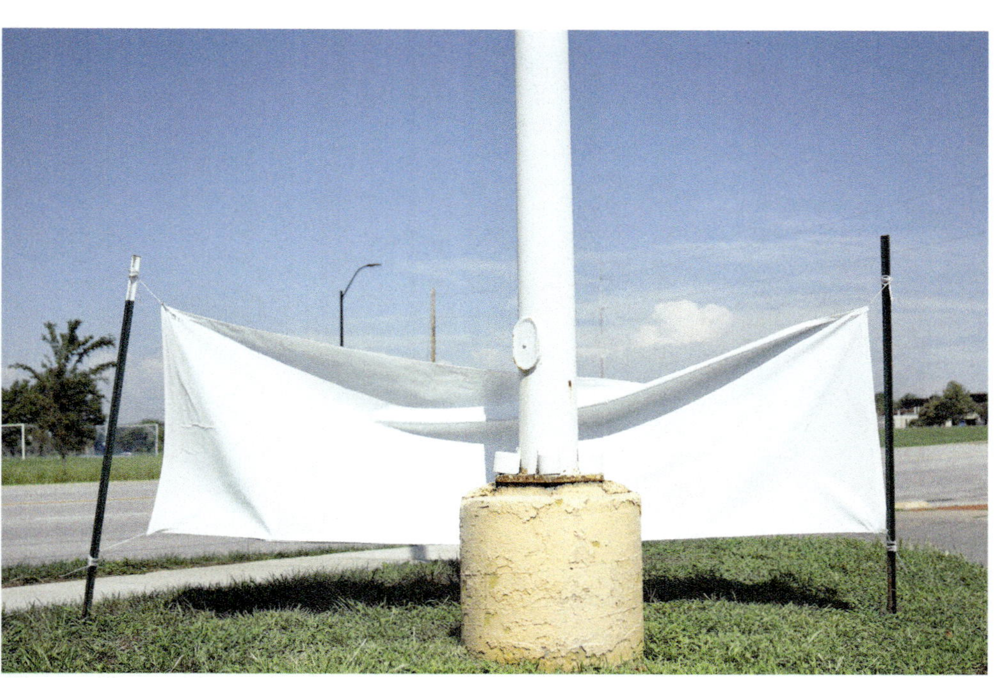

Banner, Lawrence, KS, 2018

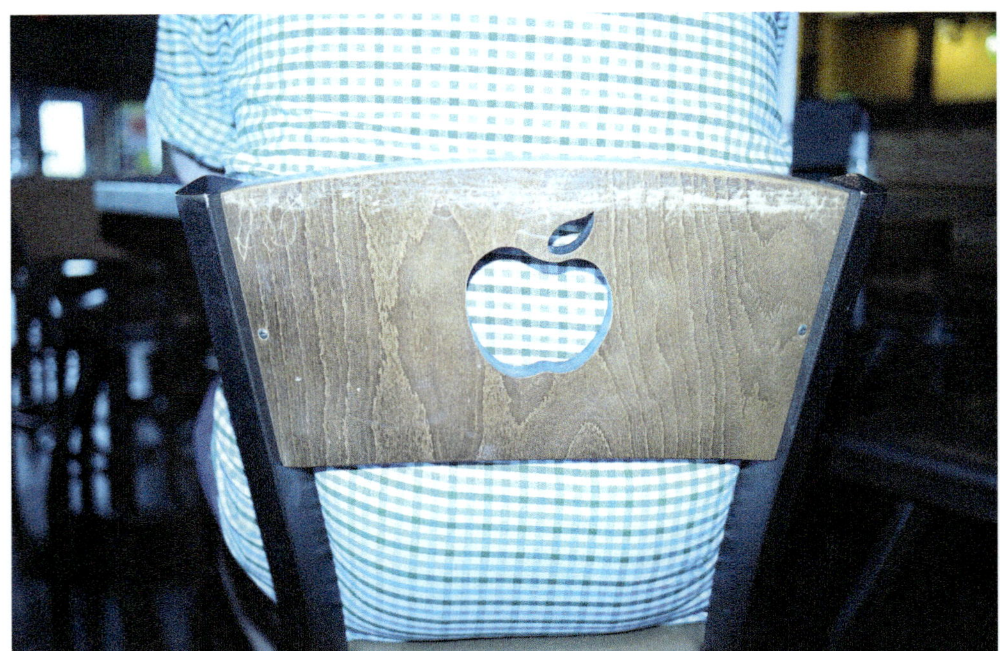

Blue Apple, Kansas City, KS, 2018

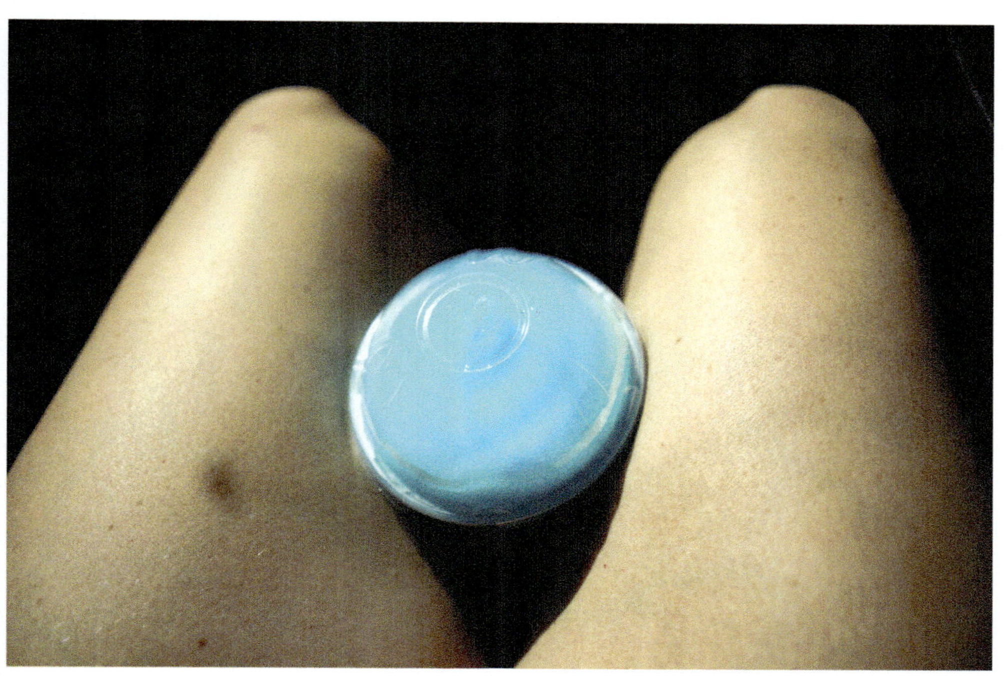

Blue Drink Between Legs with Bruise, Topeka, KS, 2018

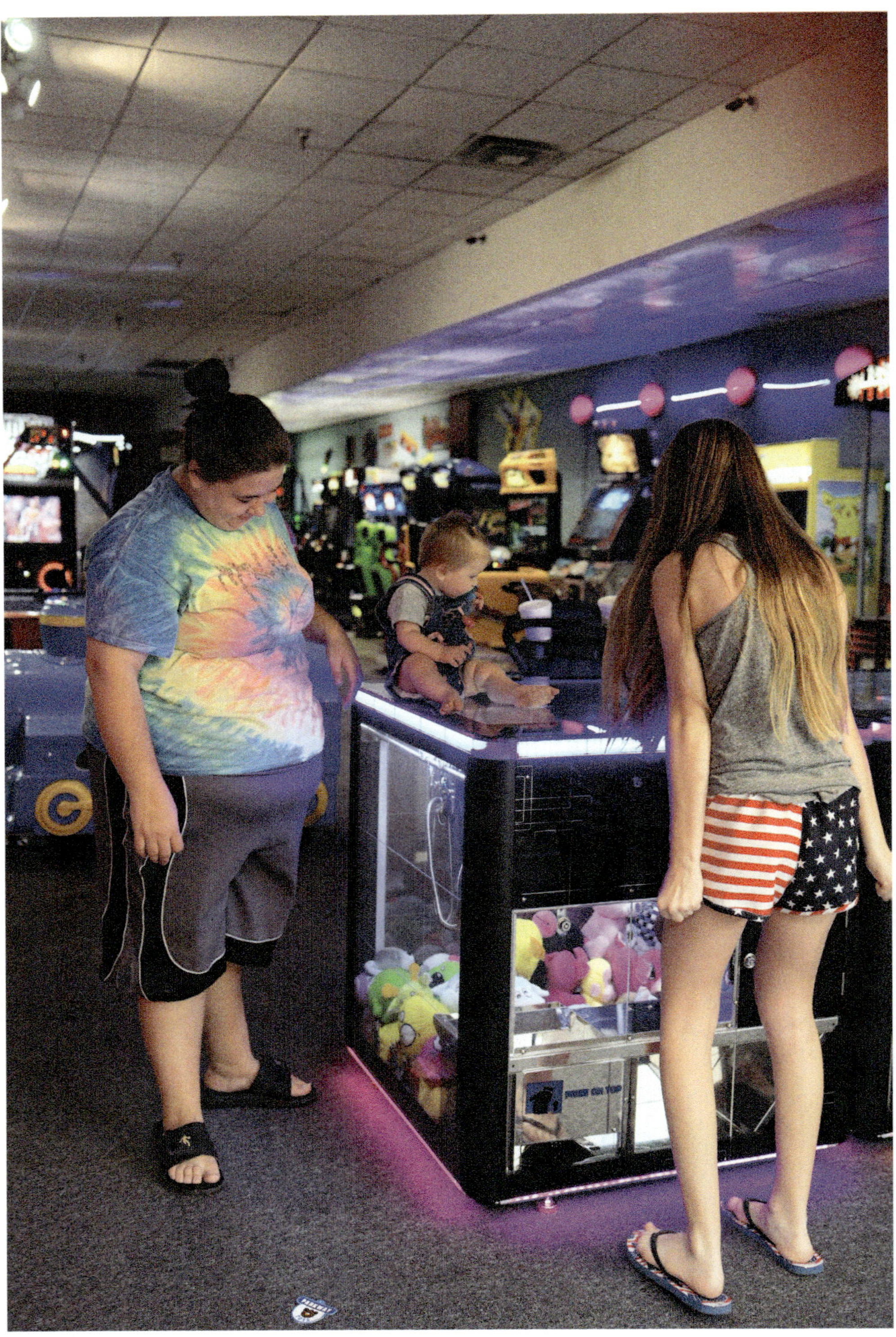

Grabber Machine, Topeka, KS, 2018

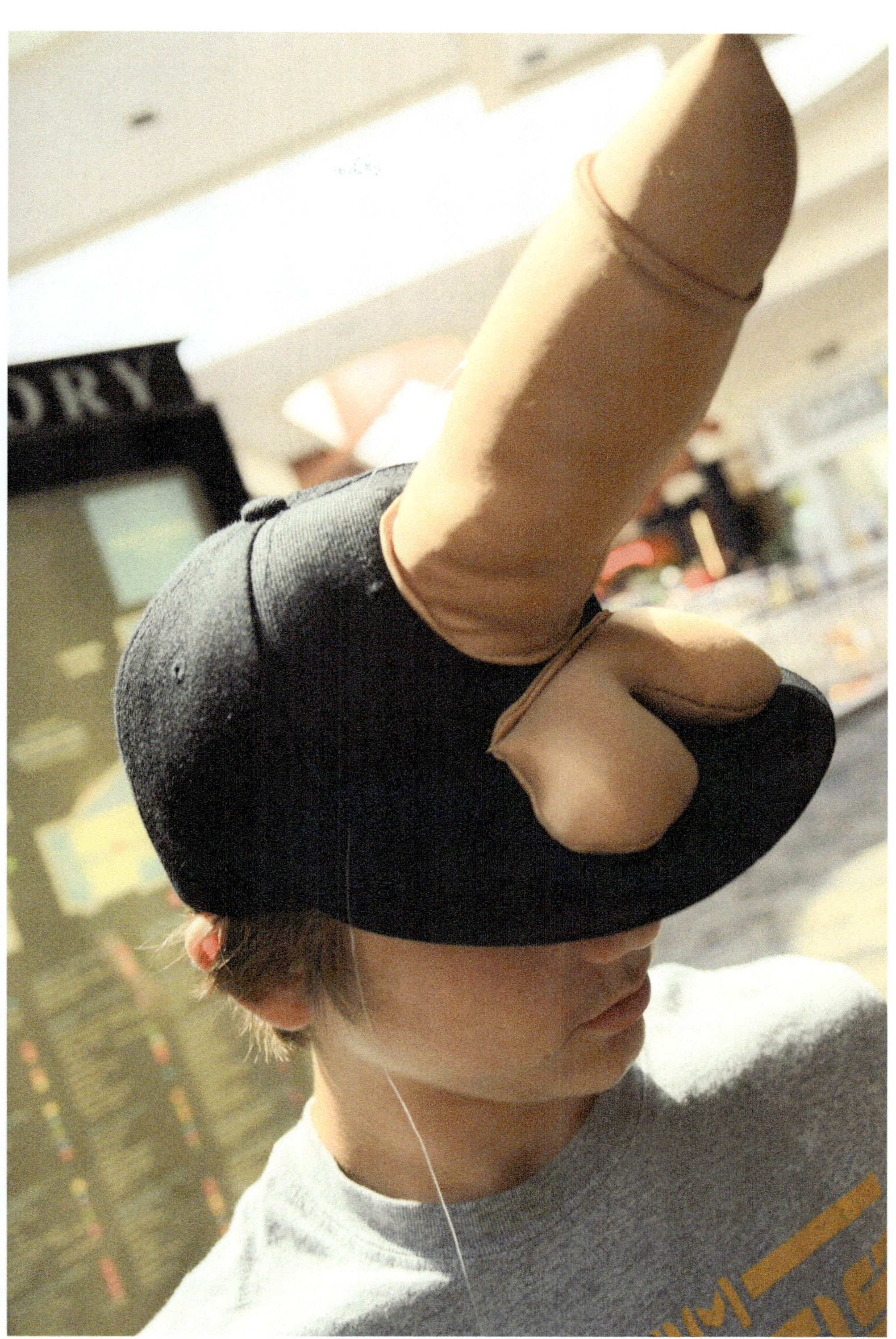

Dick Hat, Topeka, KS, 2018

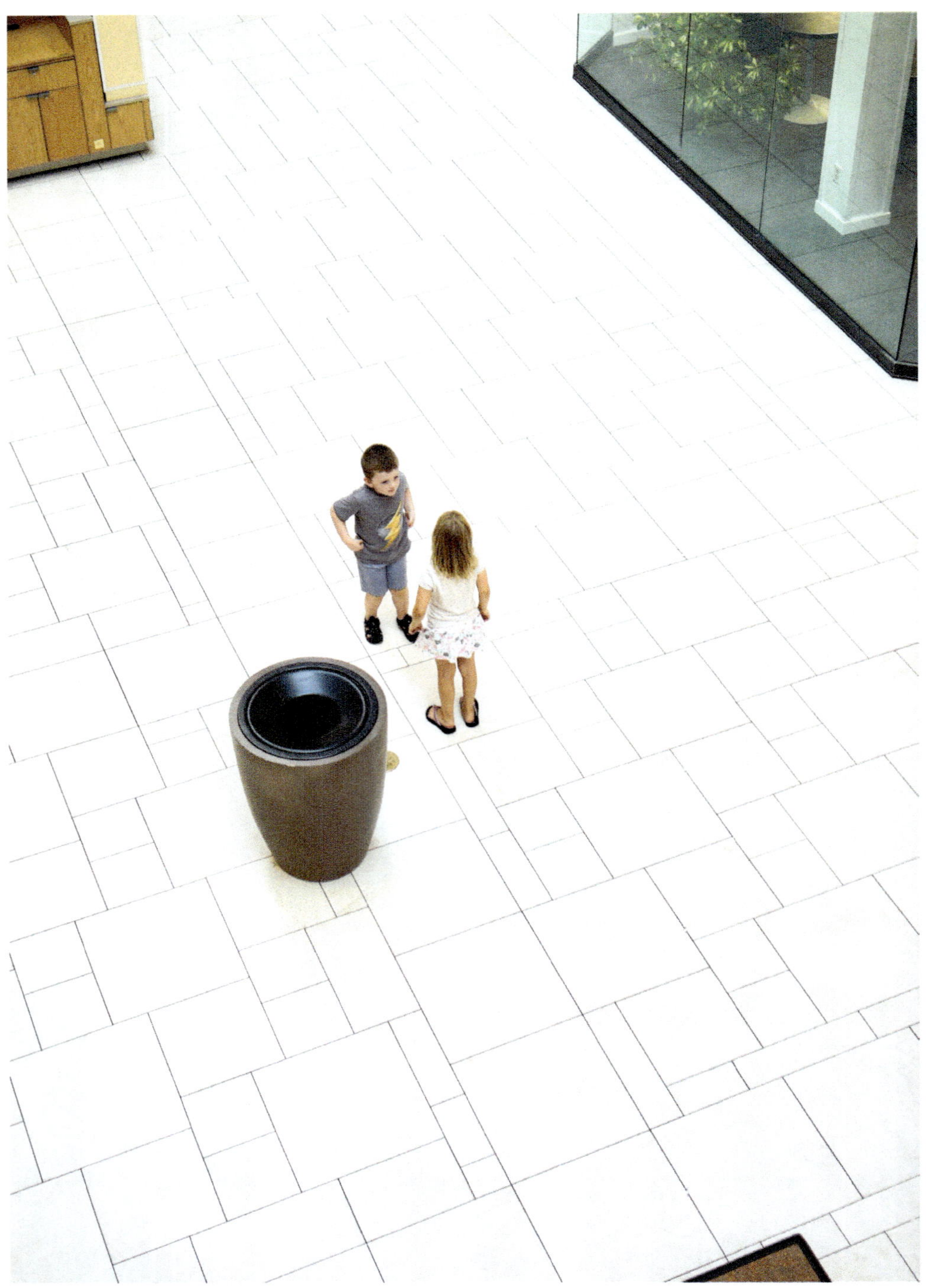

Mall Kids, Topeka, KS, 2018

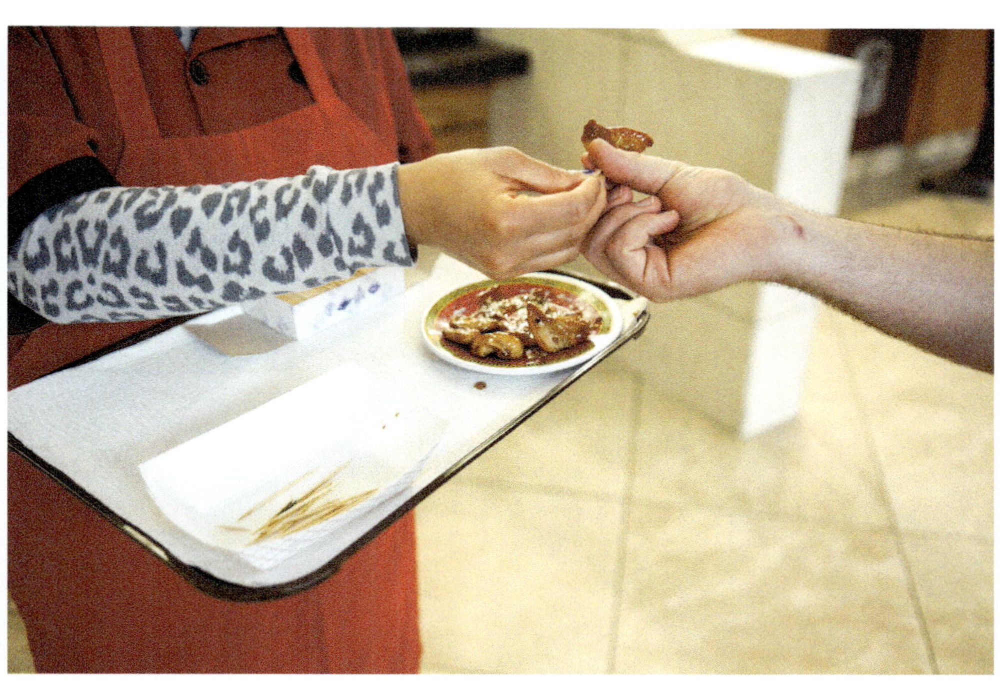

Sample Station, Topeka, KS, 2018

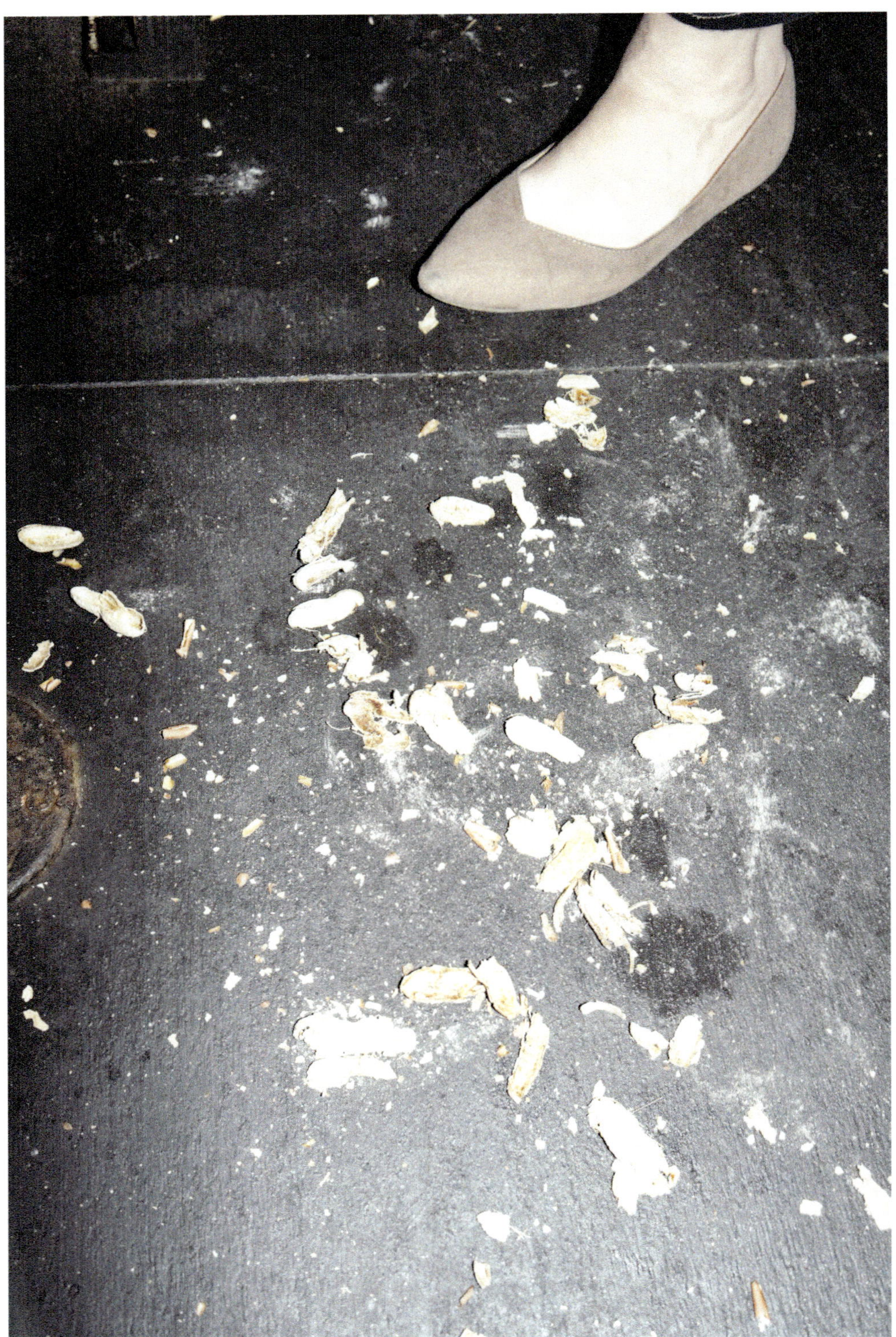

Peanuts, Lawrence, KS, 2018

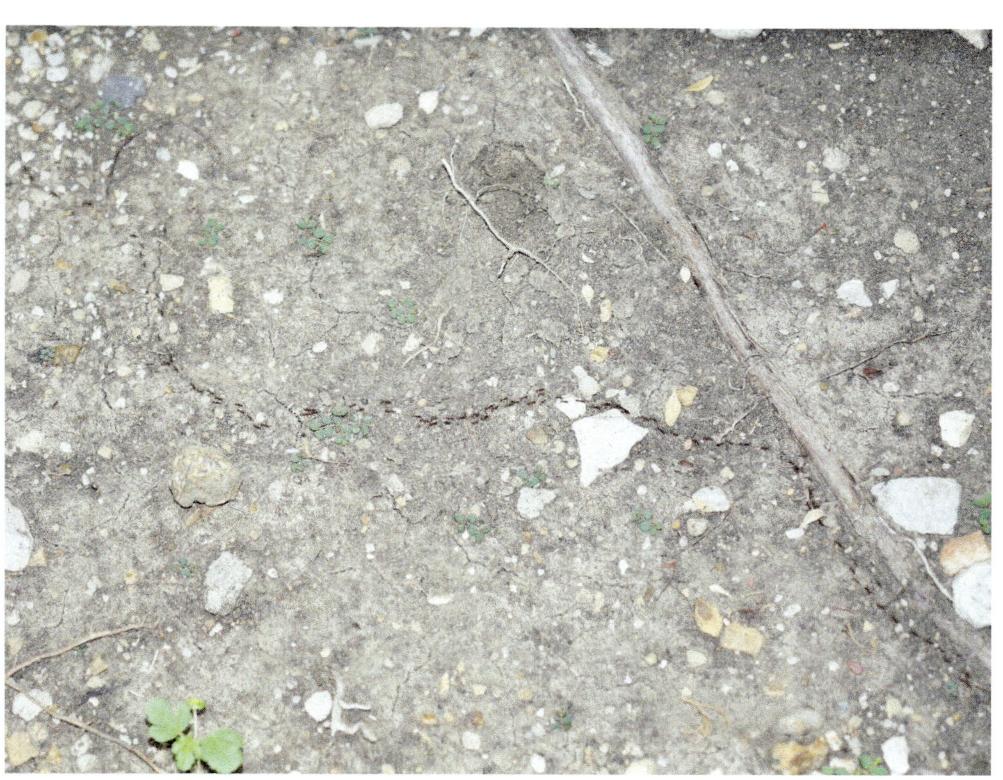
Ants, Topeka, KS, 2018

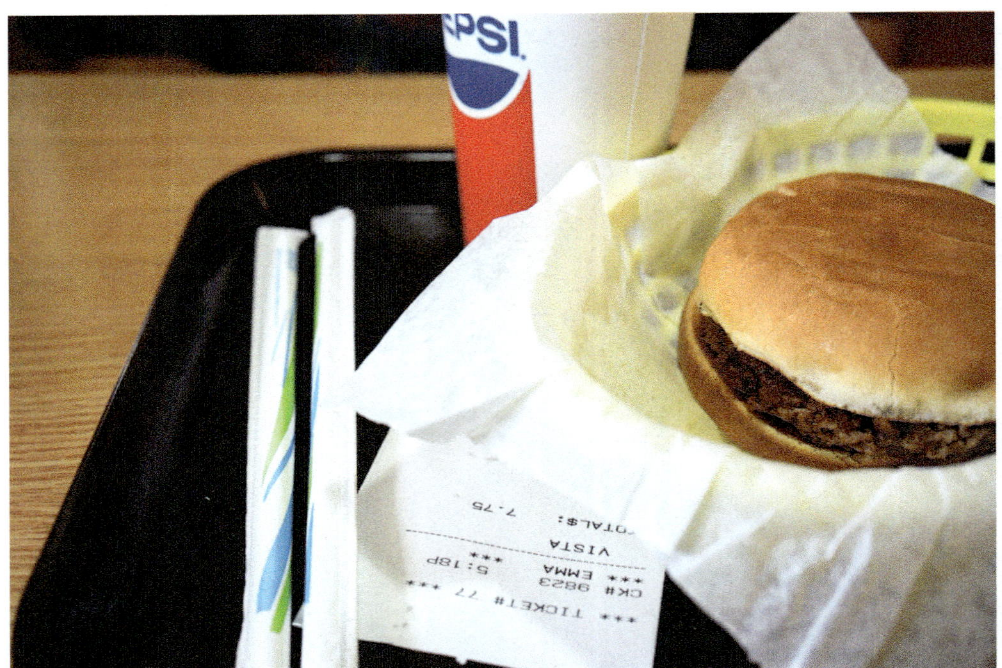

Hamburger Basket, Manhattan, KS, 2018

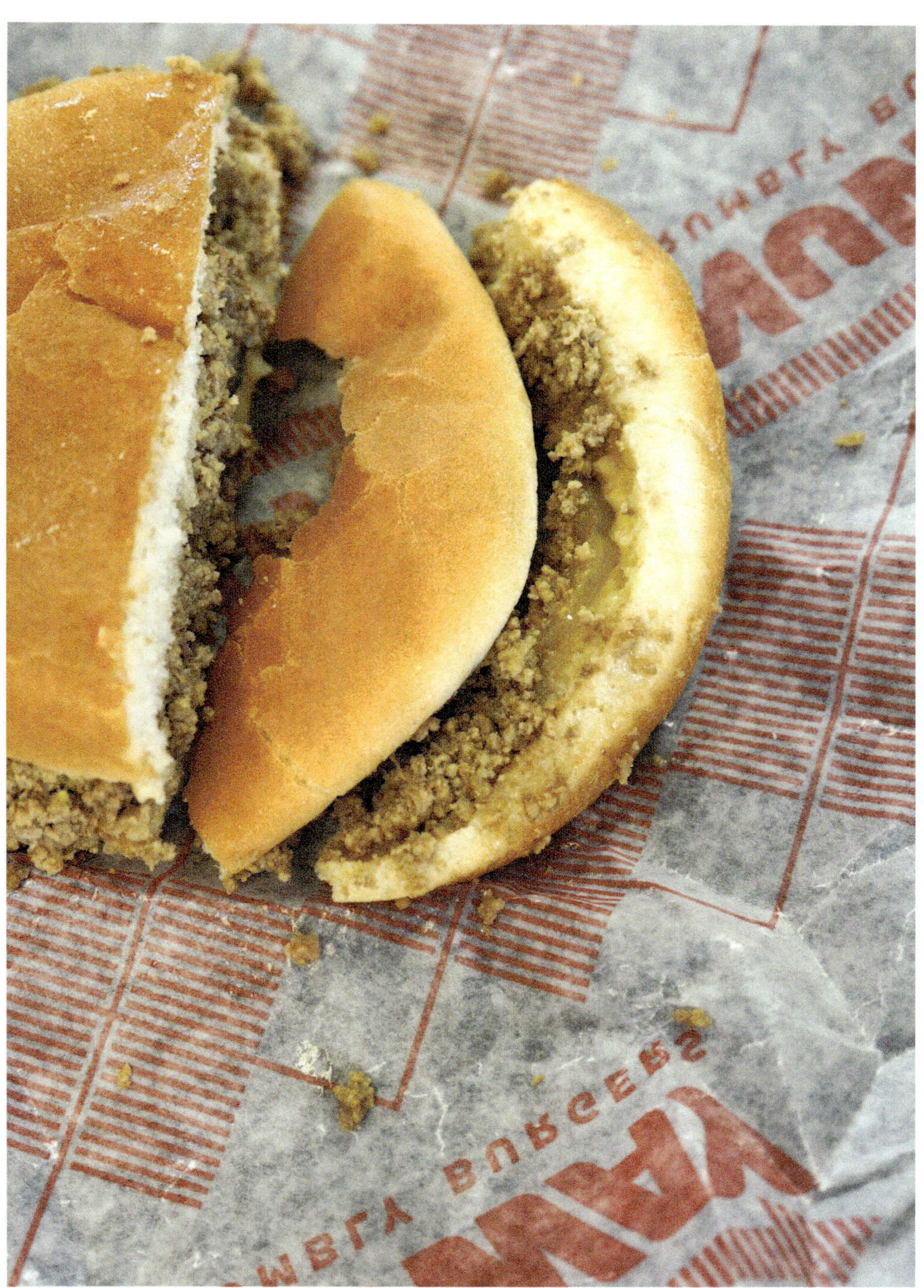

Loose Meat, Wichita, KS, 2018

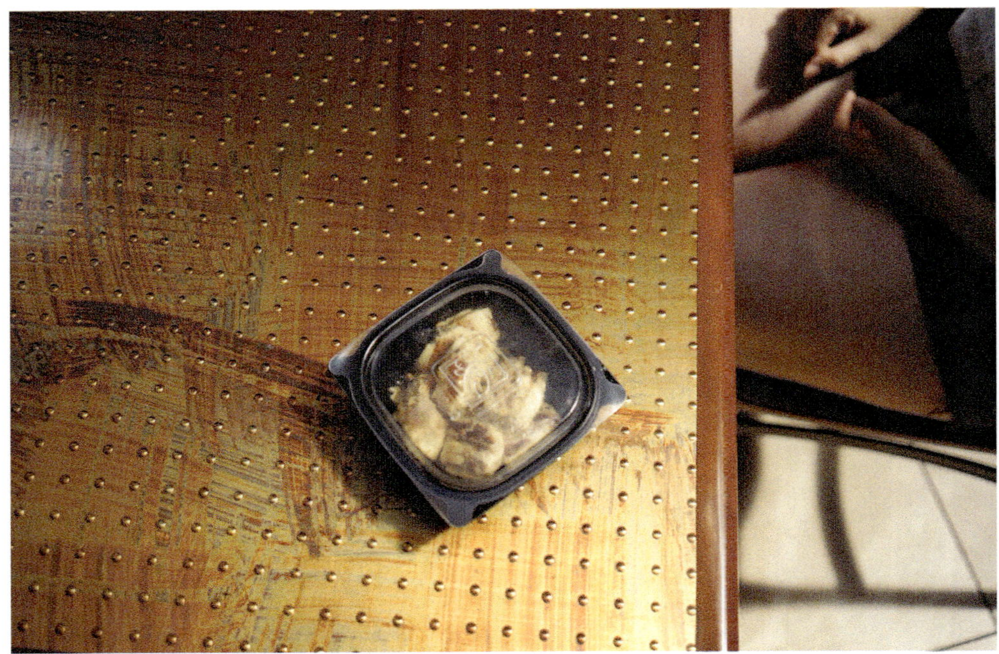

Copper Table and Chicken Nuggets, Topeka, KS, 2018

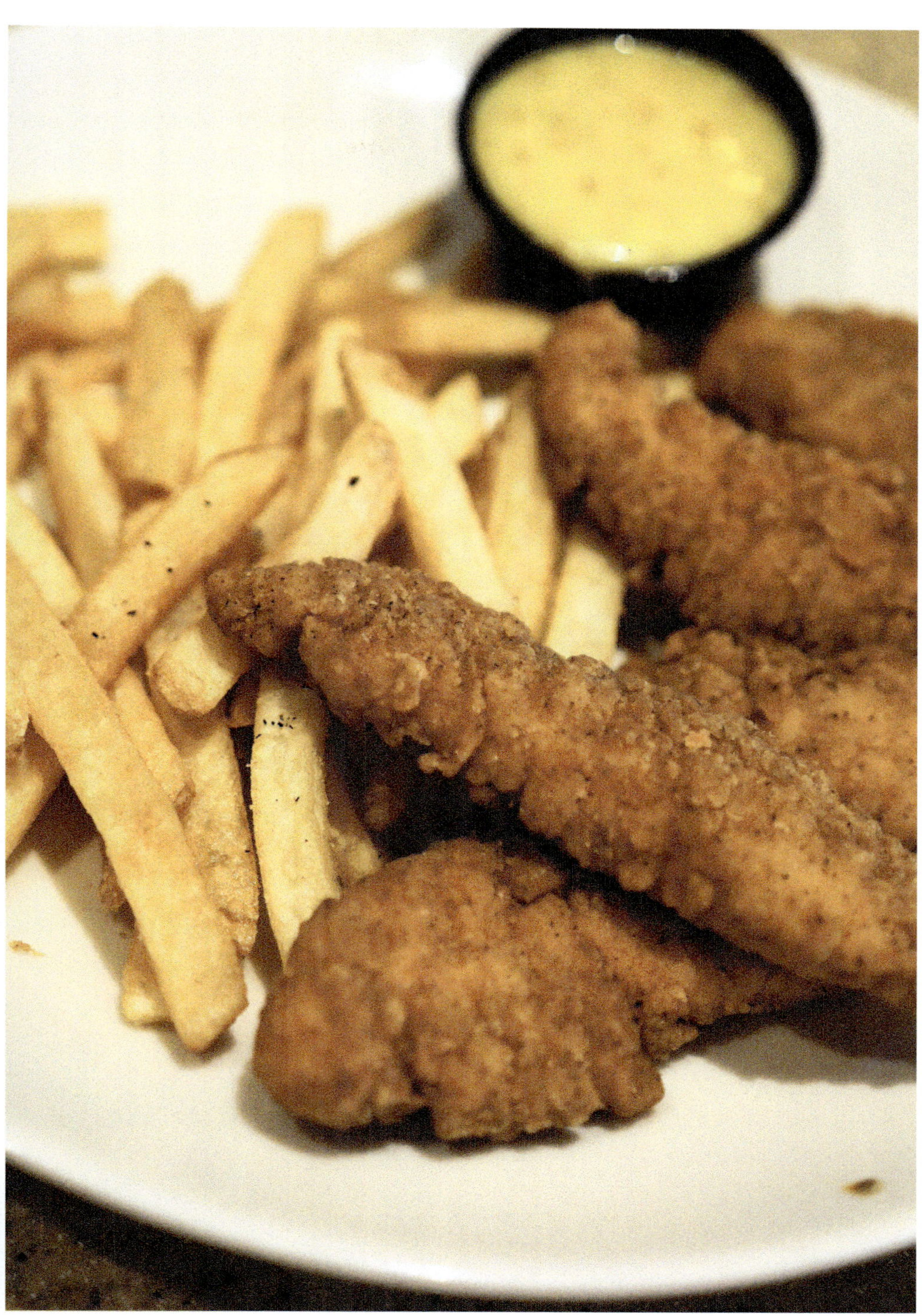

Tenders, Kansas City, KS, 2018

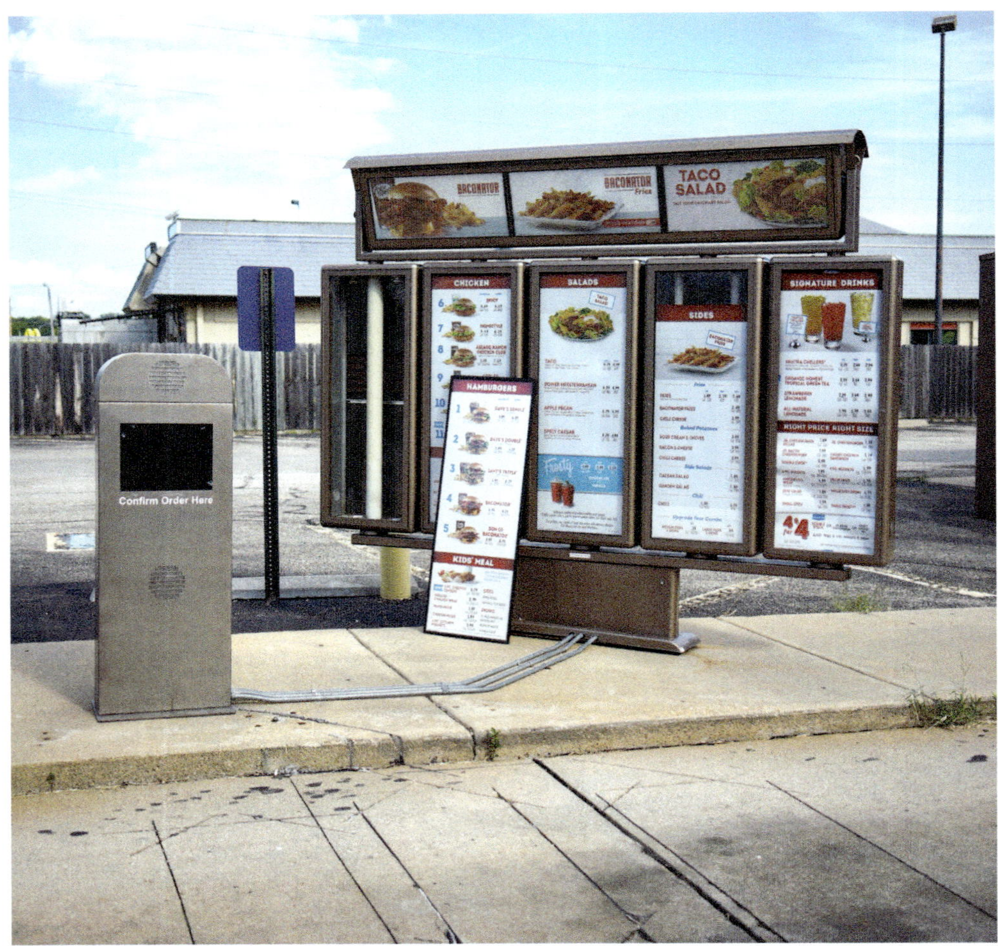

Drive-Thru With Broken Sign, Manhattan, KS, 2018

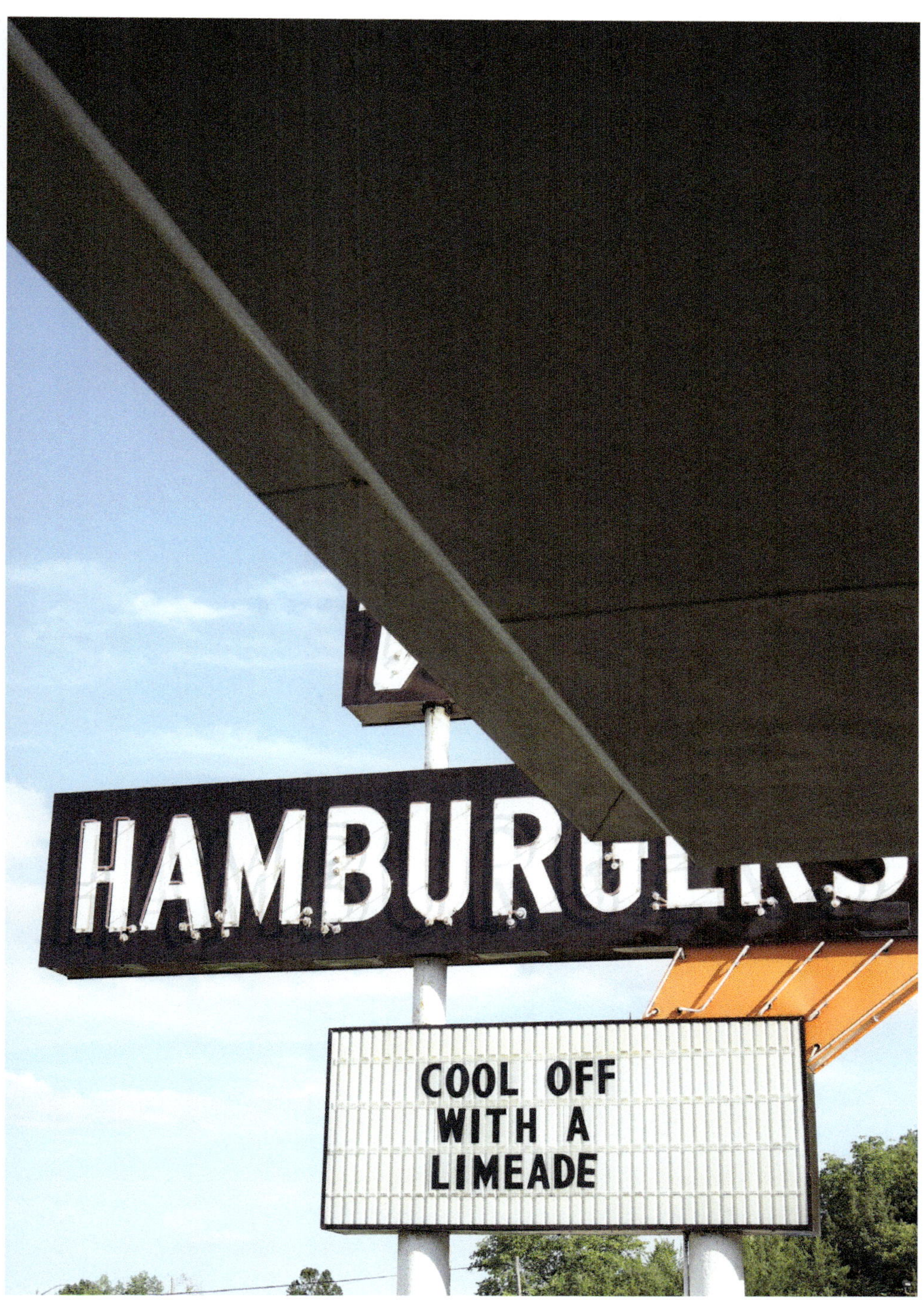

Limeade, Manhattan, KS, 2018

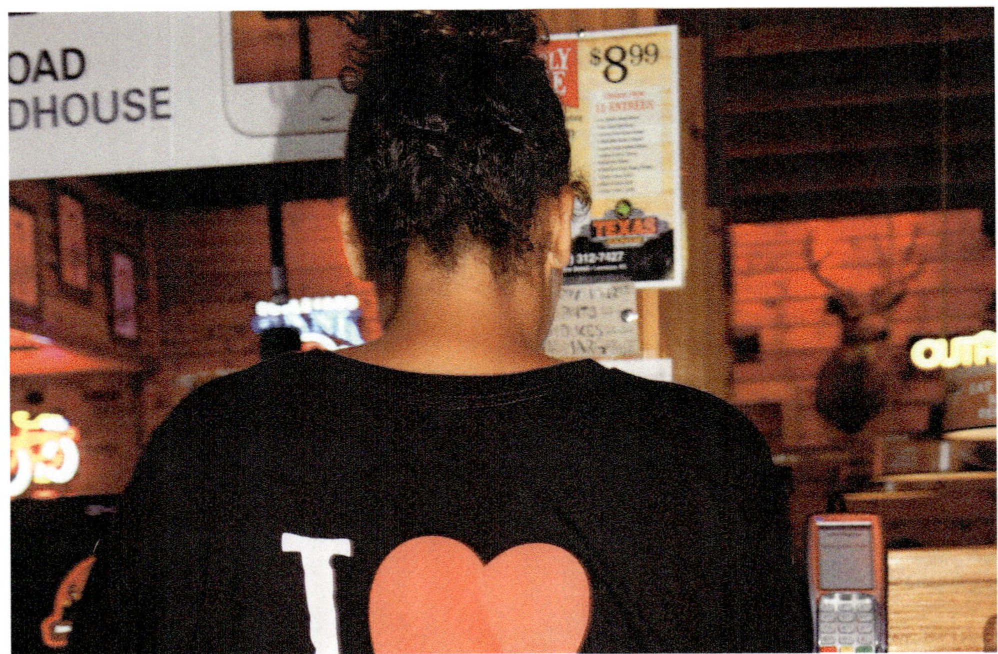

Heart, Lawrence, KS, 2018

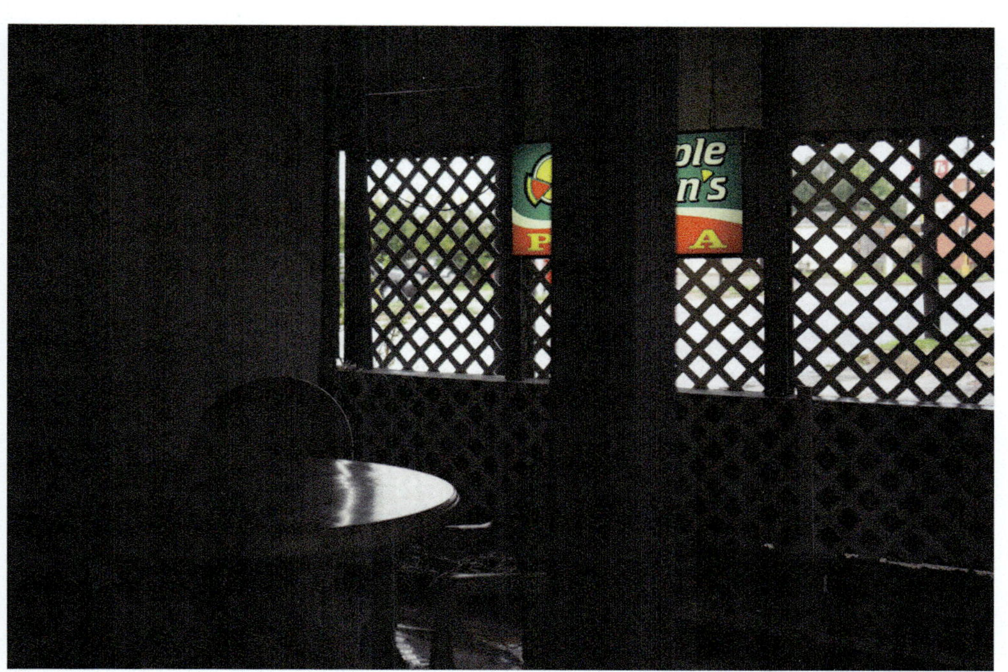

Obscured Pizza Sign, St. Joseph, MO, 2018

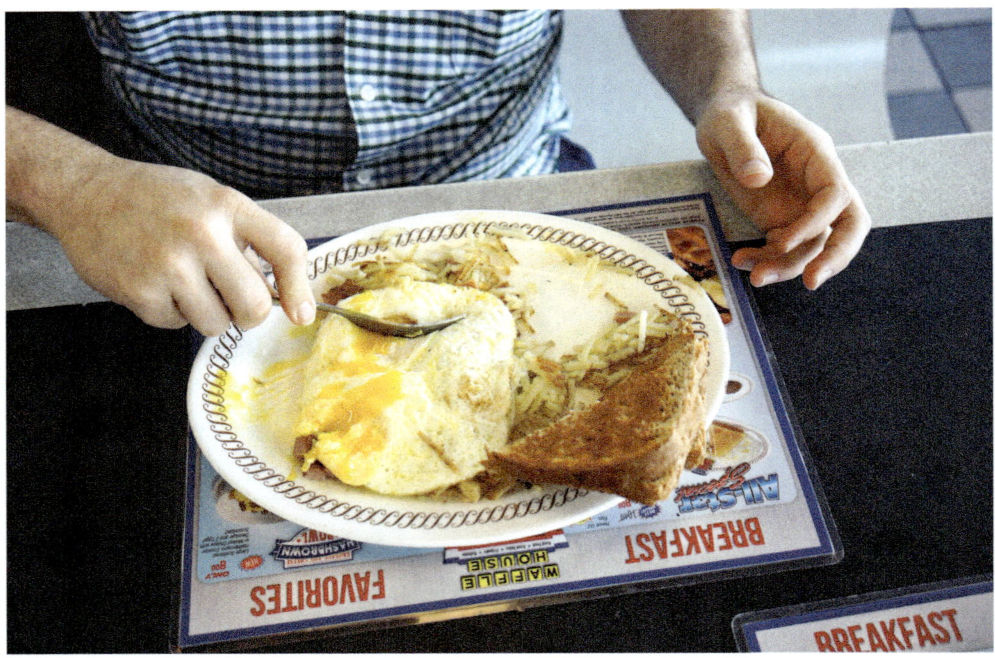

Eggs, Bonner Springs, KS, 2018

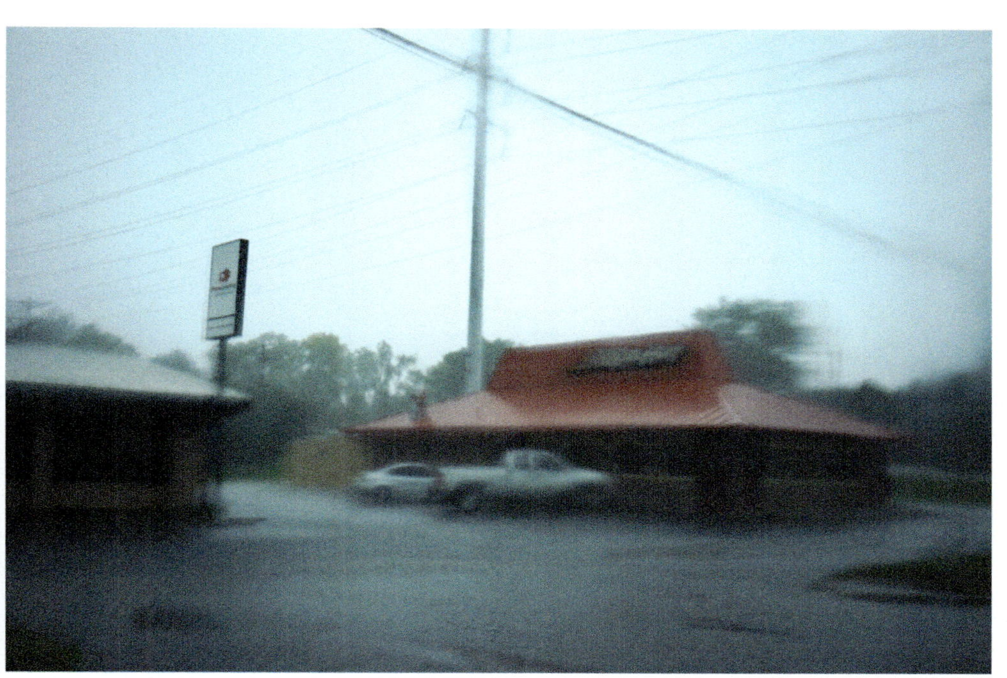

Rain, Atchison, KS, 2018

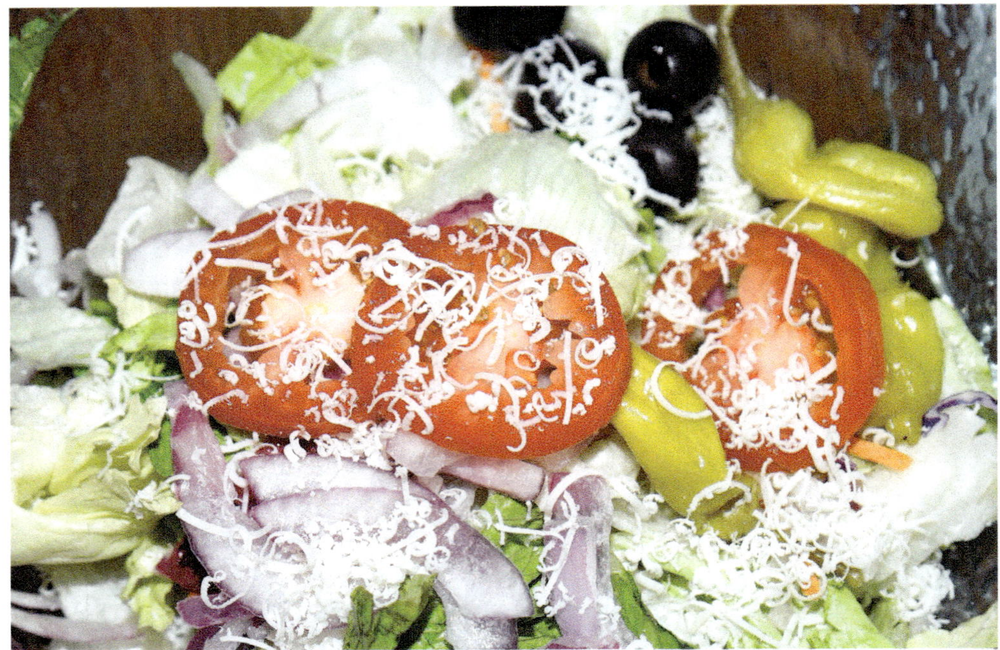

Hospitaliano #1, Topeka, KS, 2018

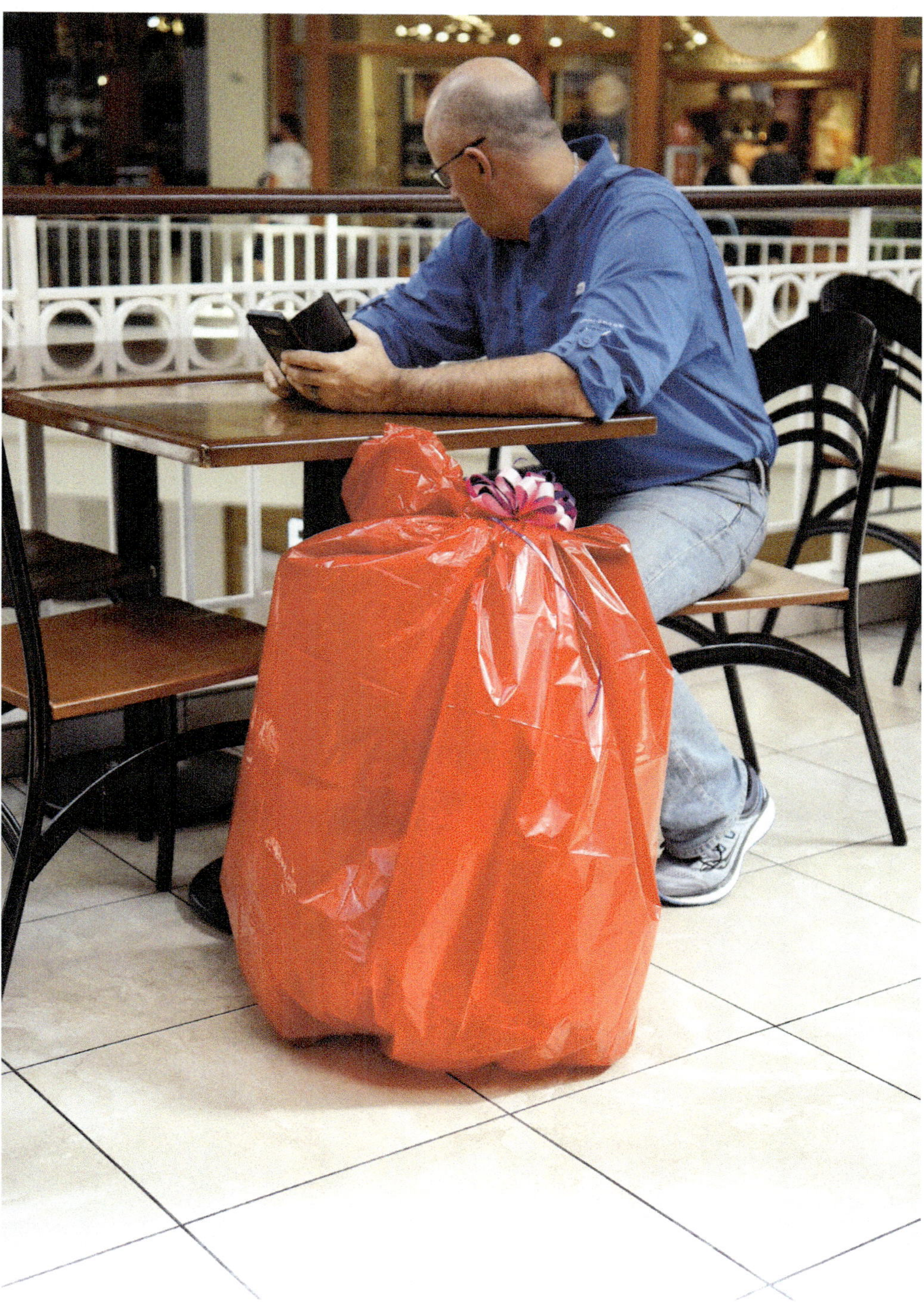

Red Bag, Topeka, KS, 2018

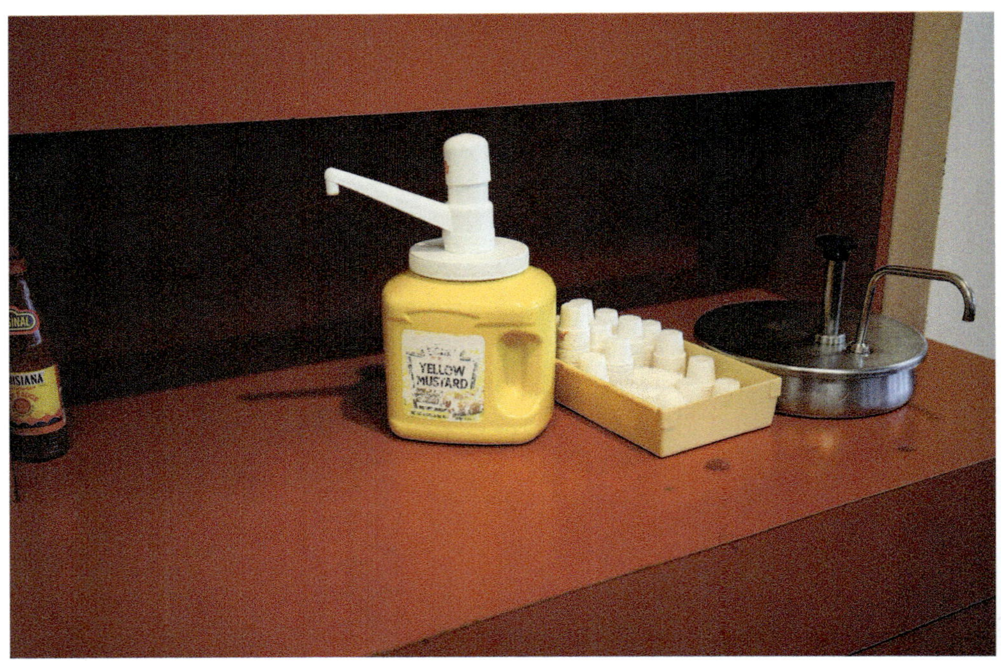

Mustard Station, Manhattan, KS, 2018

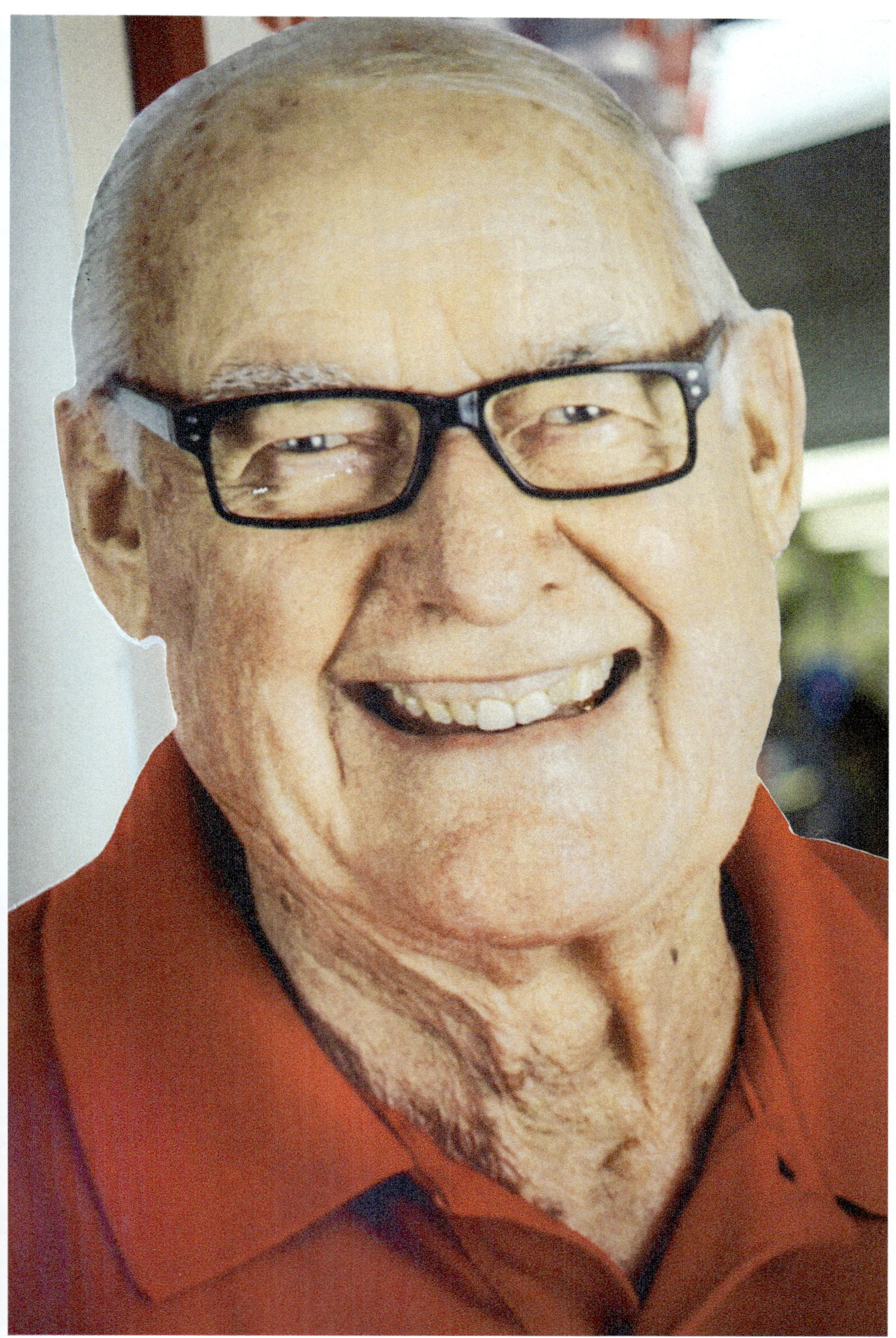

Freddy #1, El Dorado, KS, 2018

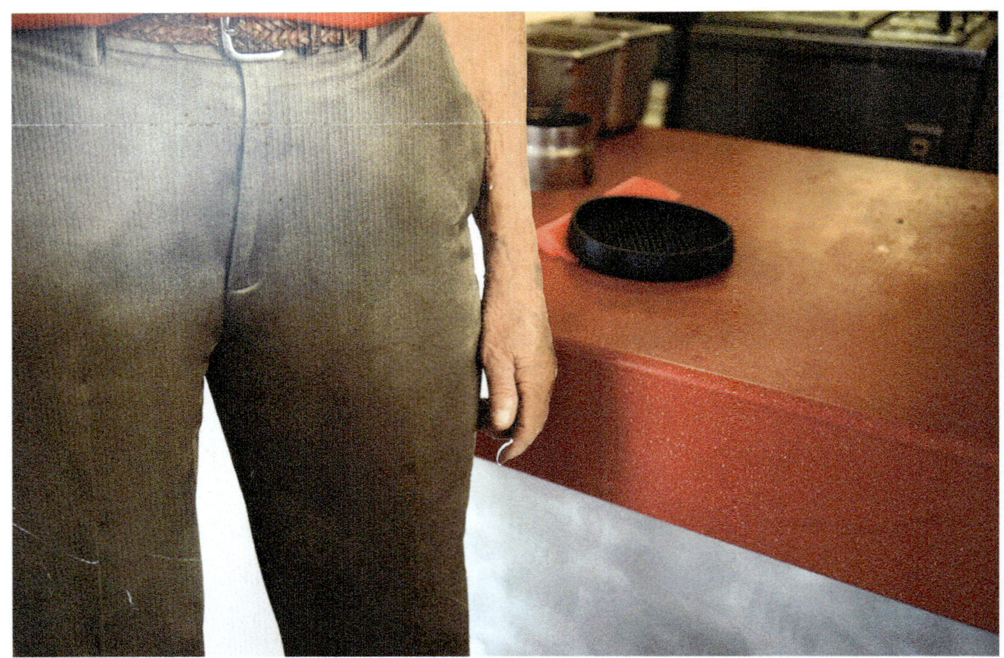

Freddy #2, El Dorado, KS, 2018

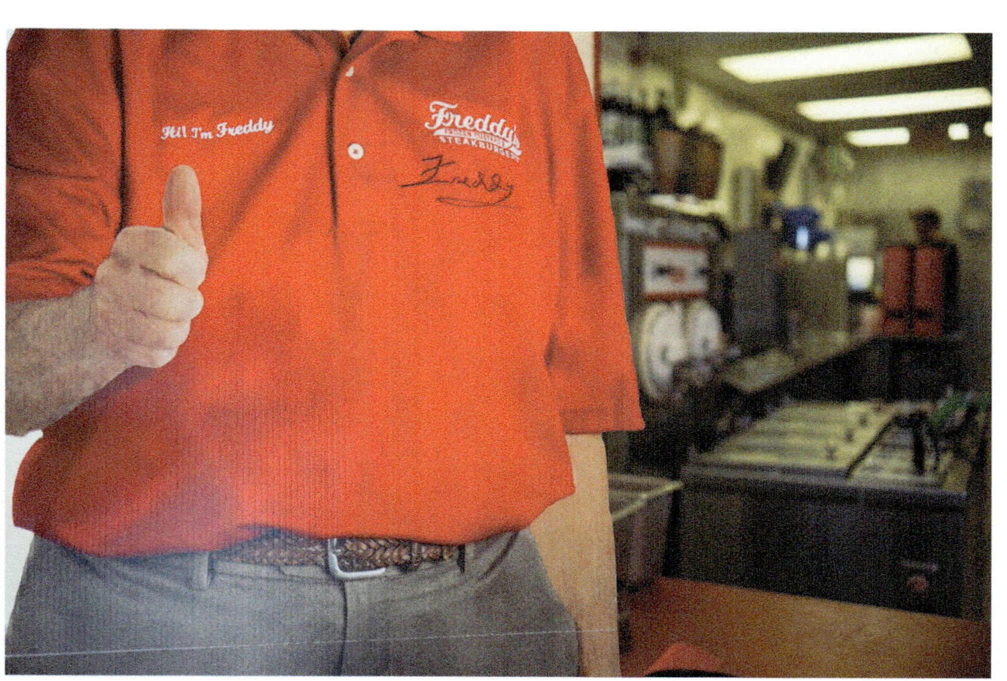

Freddy #3, El Dorado, KS, 2018

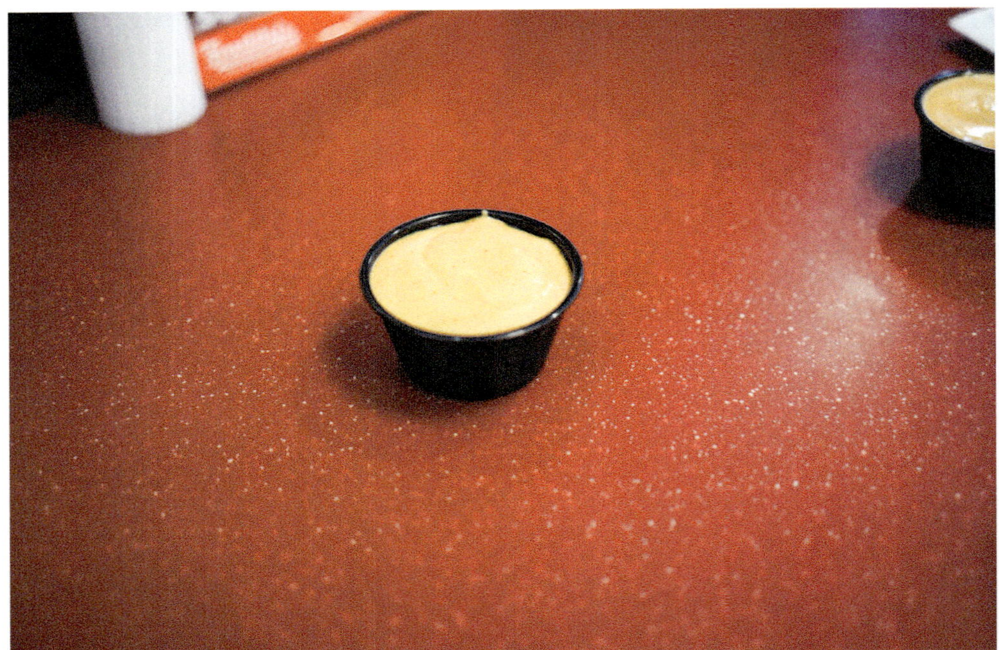

Fry Sauce, El Dorado, KS, 2018

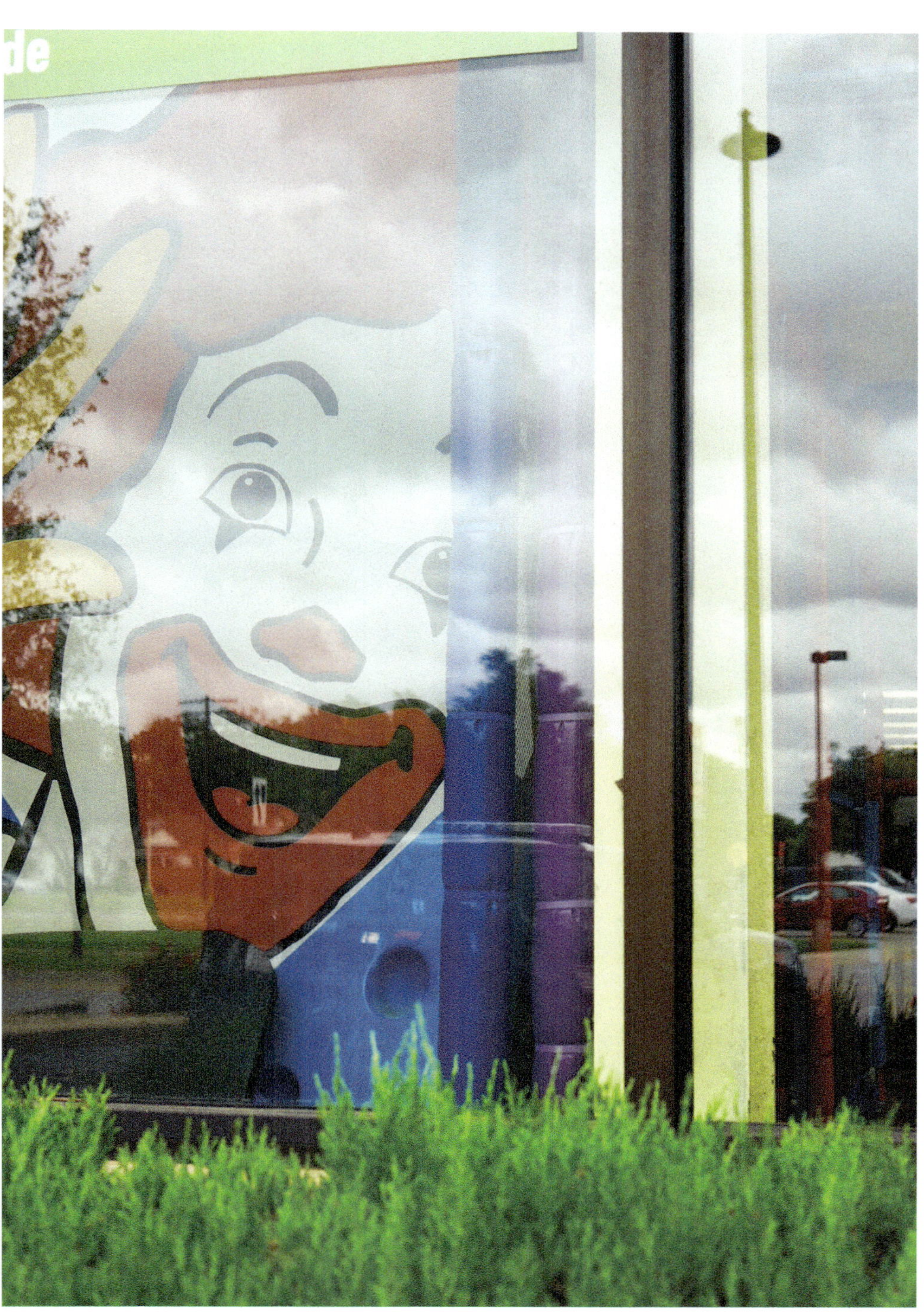

PlayPlace, Wichita, KS, 2018

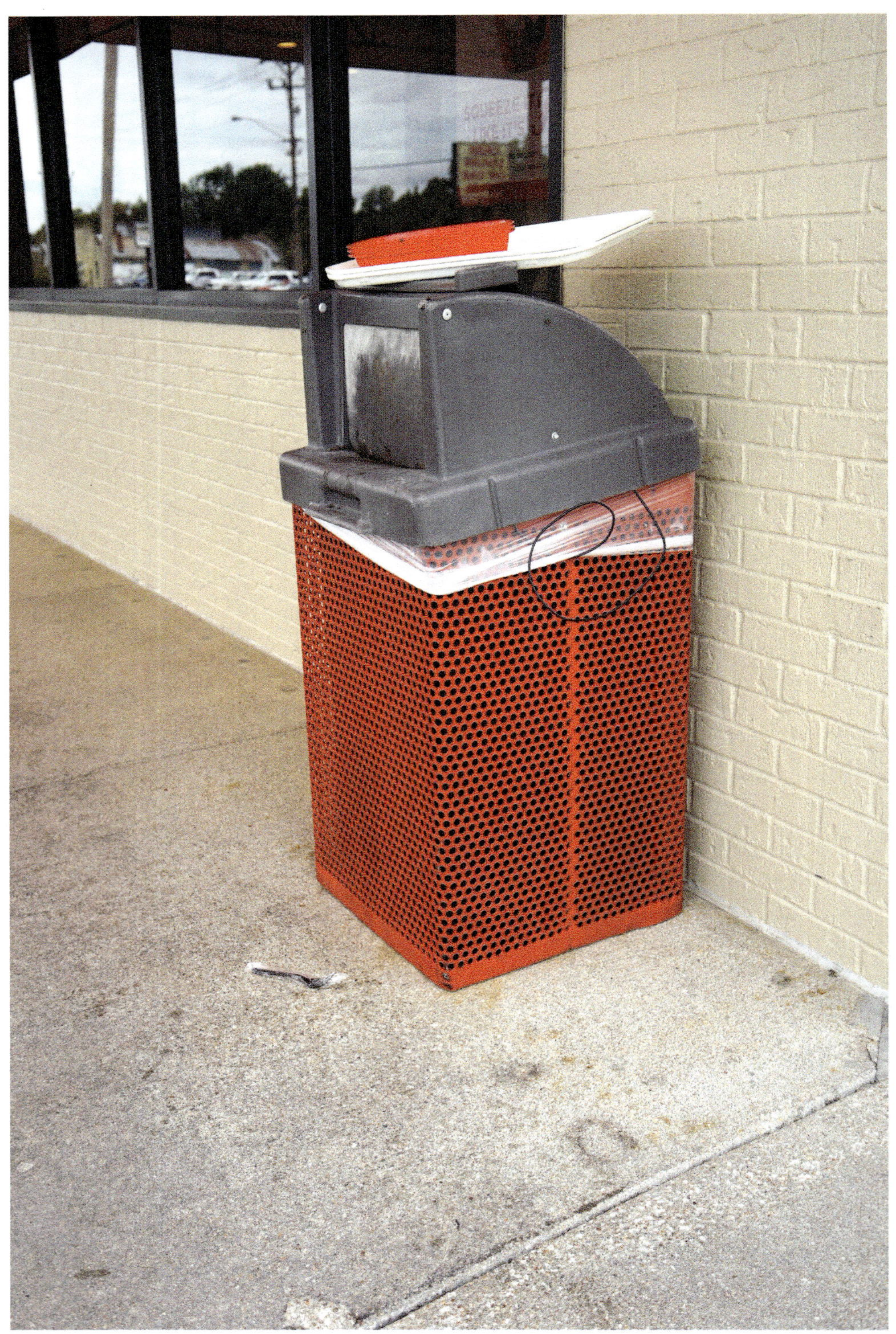

Red Can with Wire and Trays, El Dorado, KS, 2018

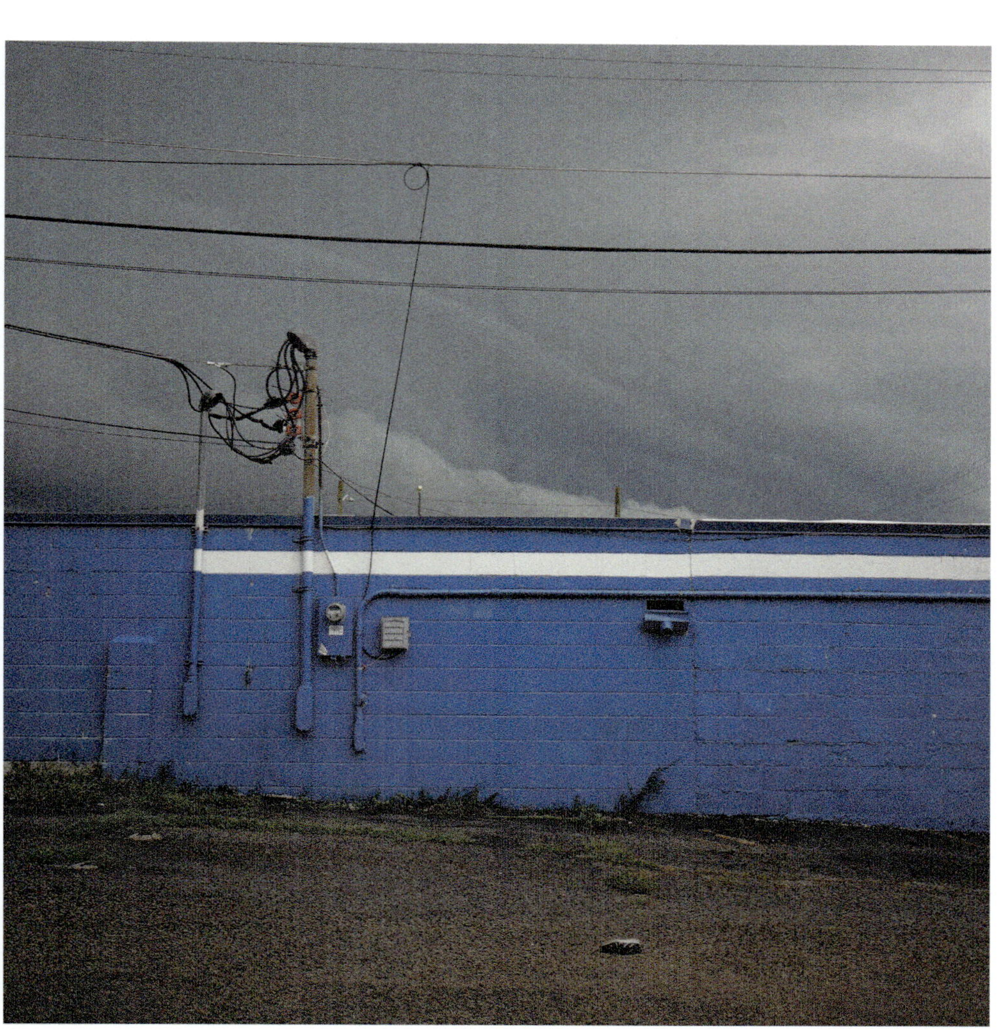

Storm with Wires, St. Joseph, MO, 2018

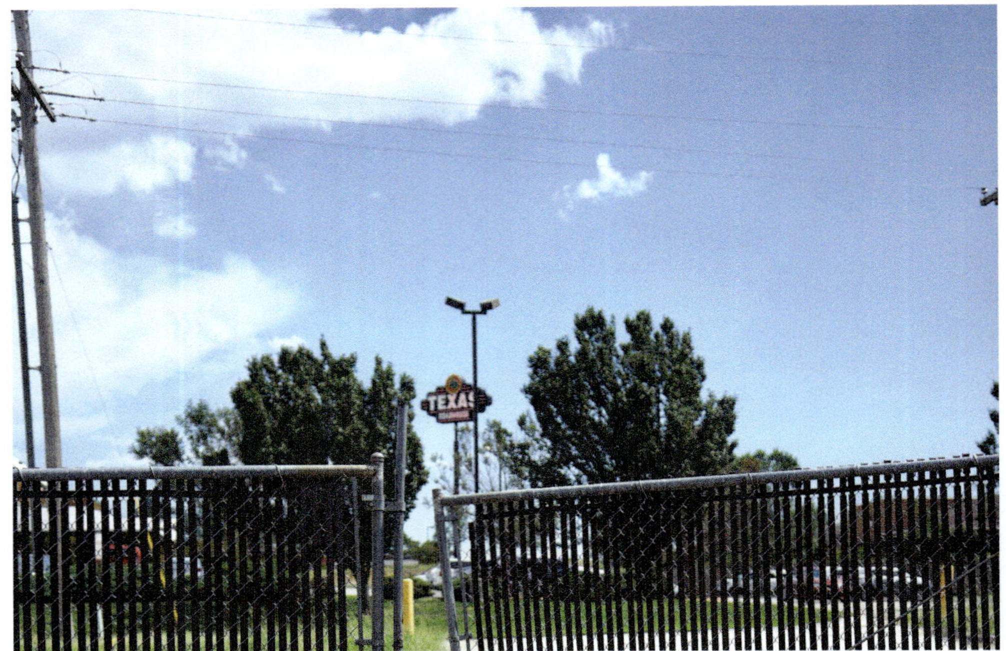

From a Parking Lot Looking in the Direction of Texas Roadhouse, Topeka, KS, 2018

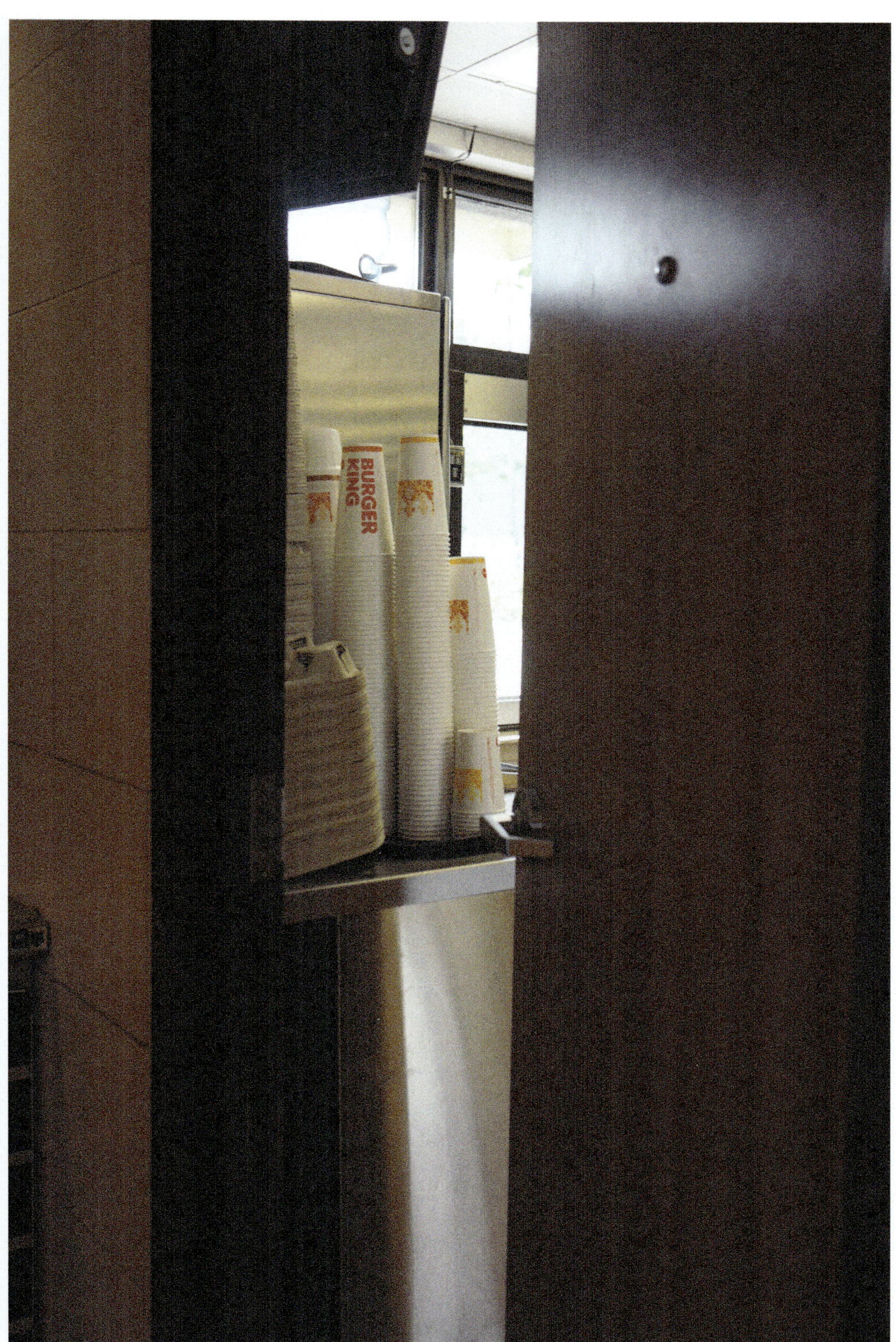

Cup Towers, Lawrence, KS, 2018

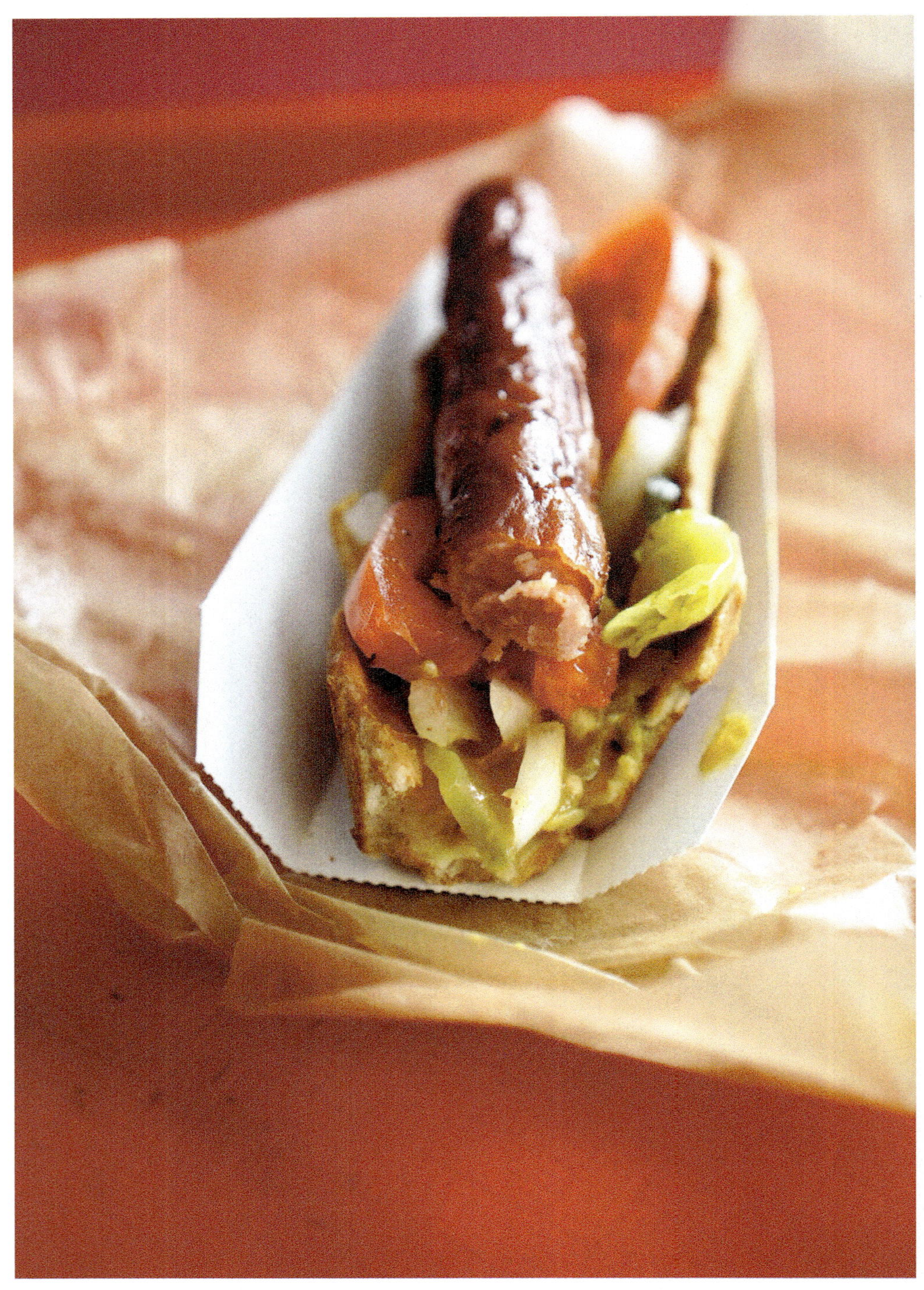

Chicago Dog #1, Wichita, KS, 2018

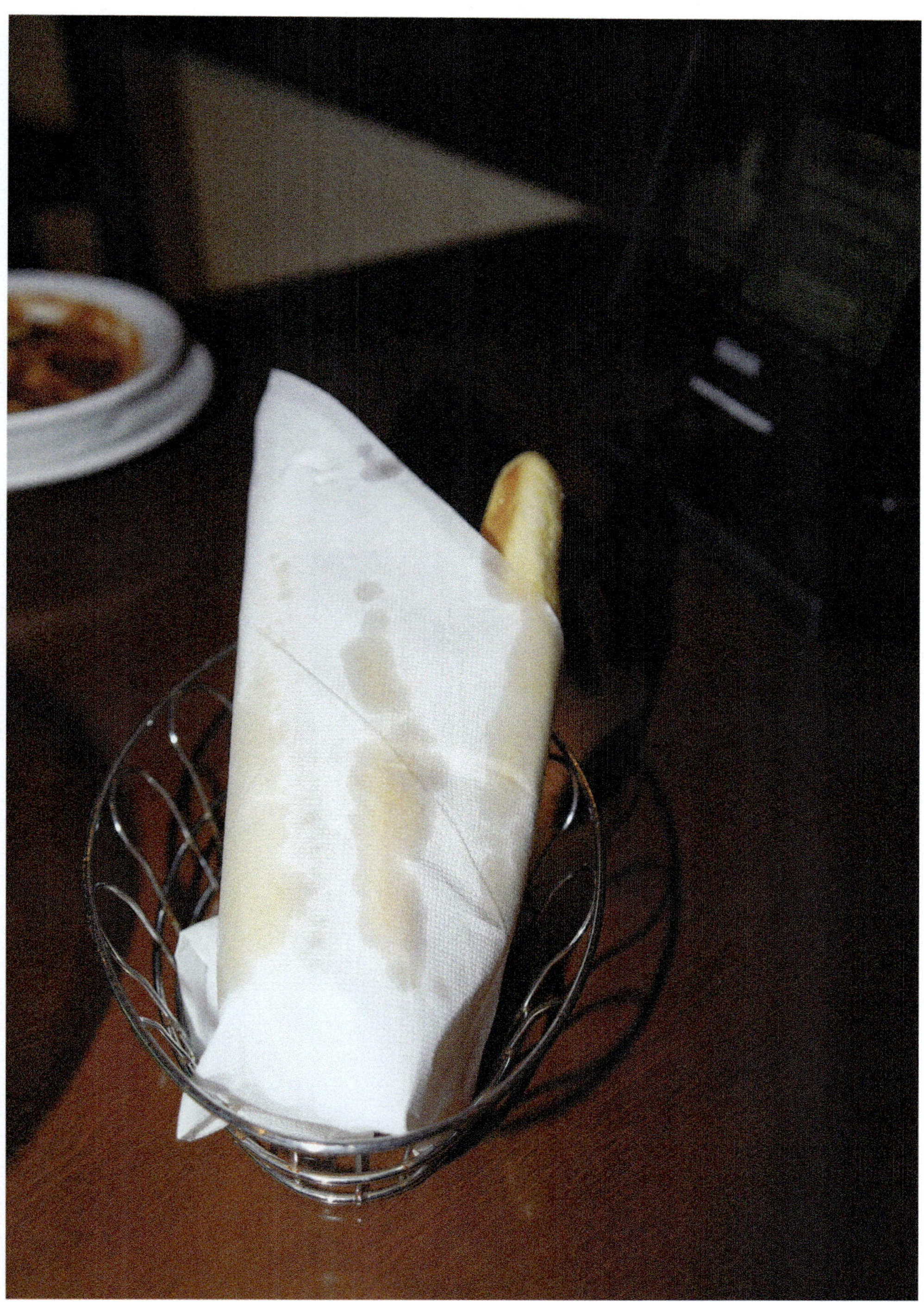

Hospitaliano #2, Topeka, KS, 2018

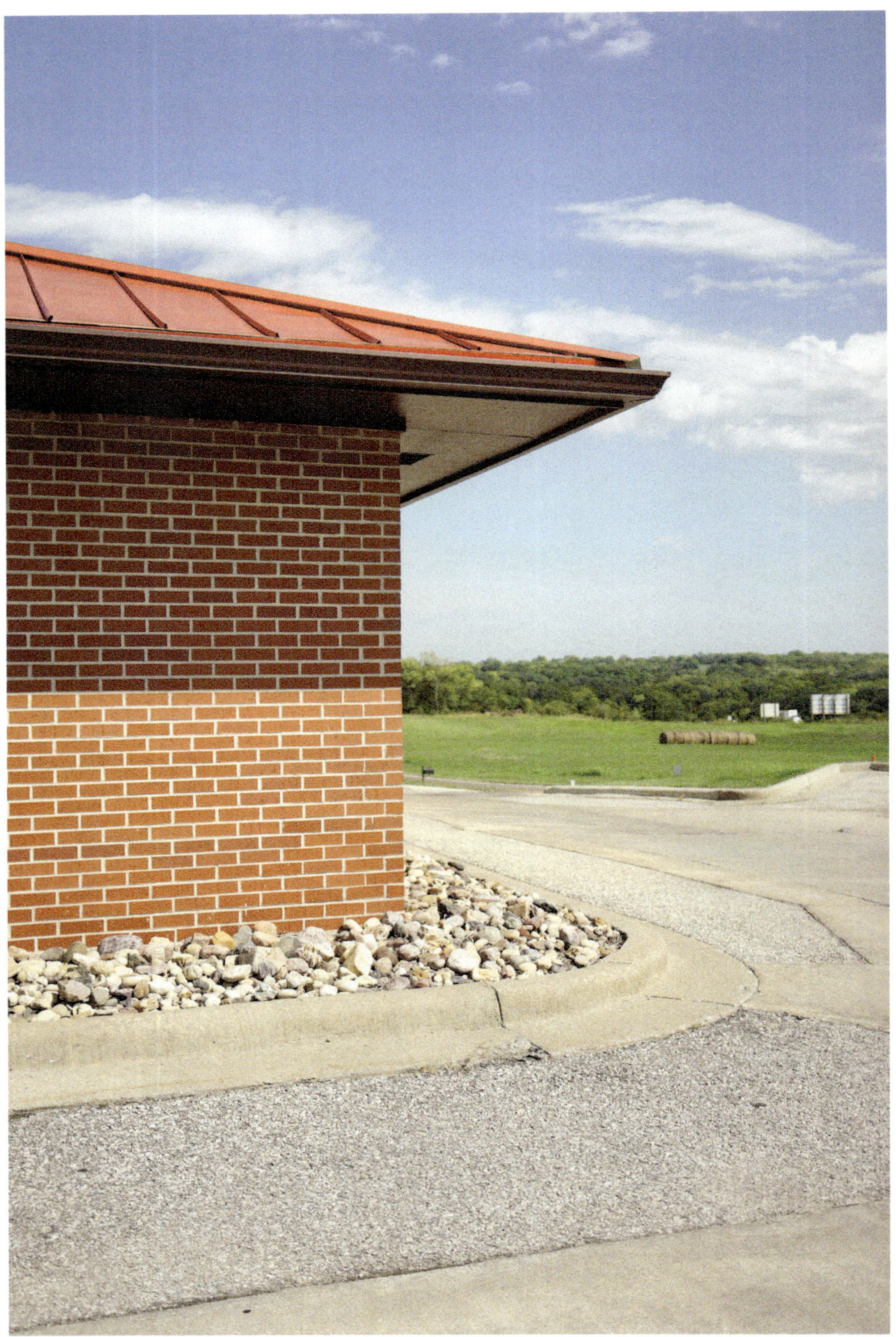

Hay Bales with Pizza Roof, De Soto, KS, 2018

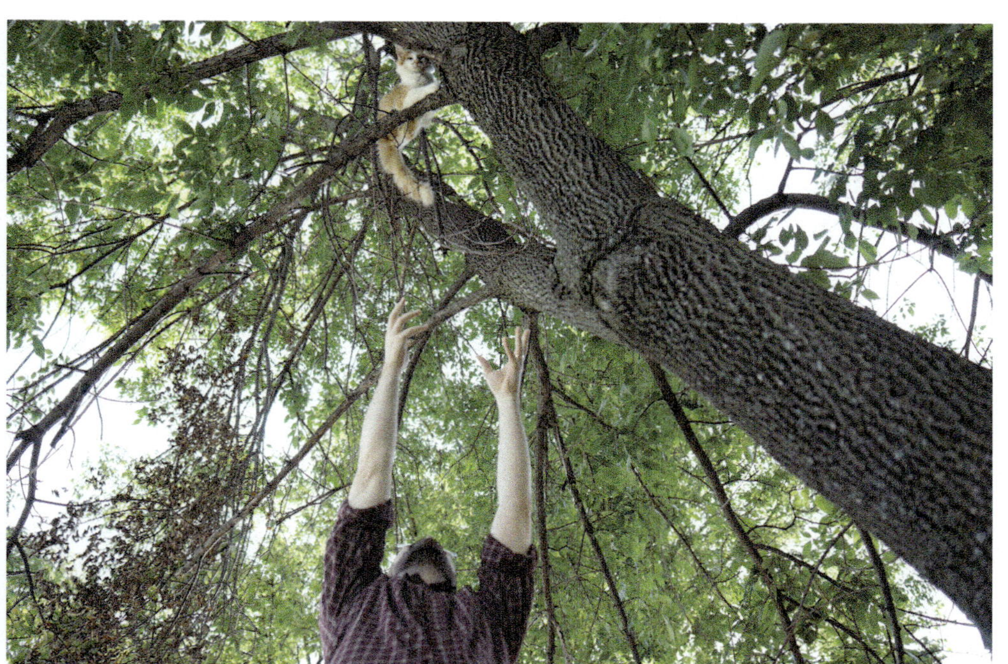

Poet with Cat in Tree, Lawrence, KS, 2018

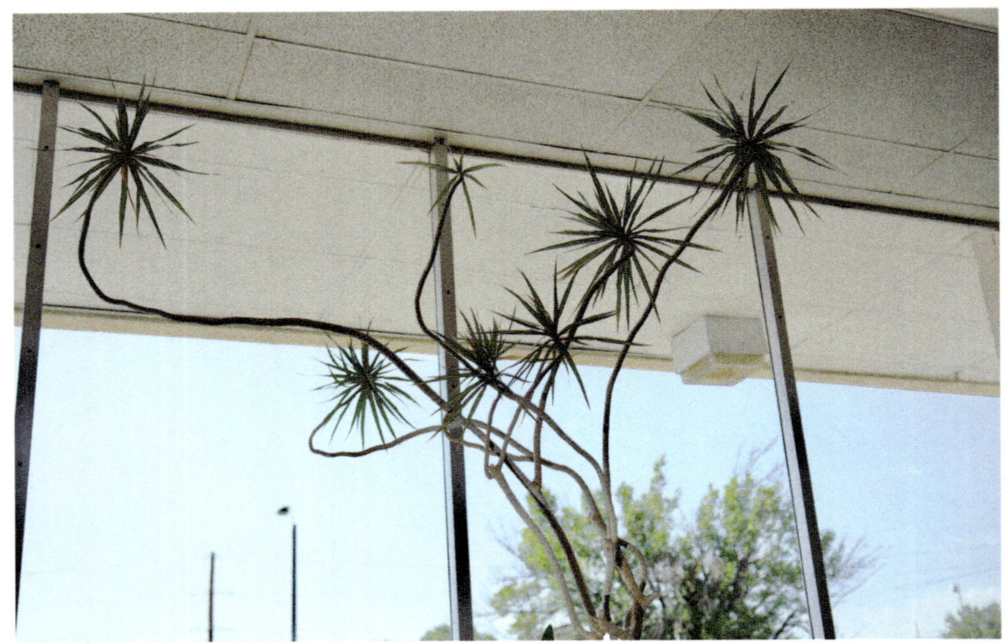

Greenery, Lawrence, KS, 2018

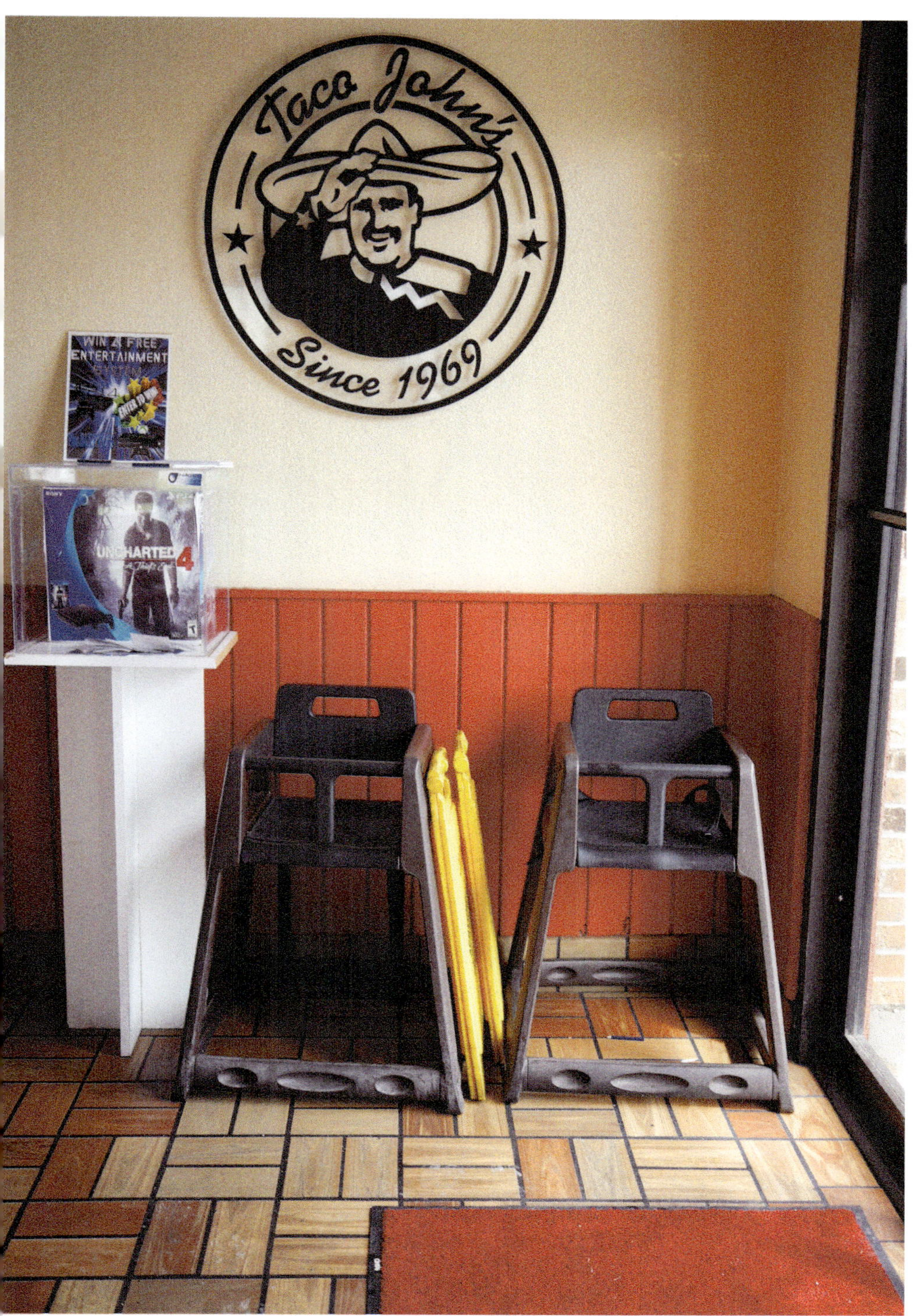

Plastic High Chairs, Atchison, KS, 2018

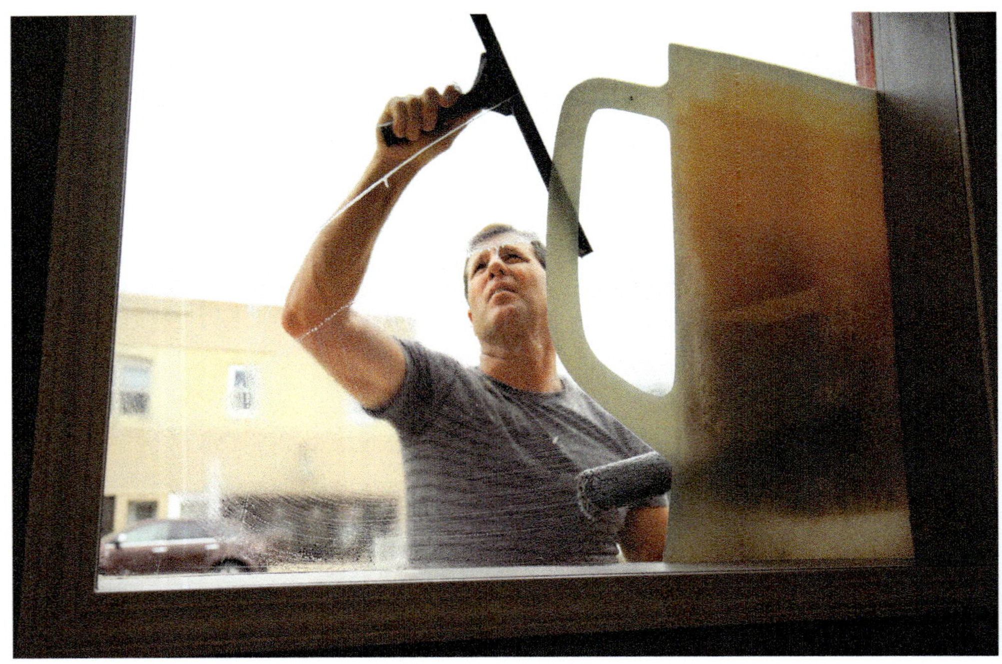

Window Washer and Large Root Beer Stein, Wichita, KS, 2018

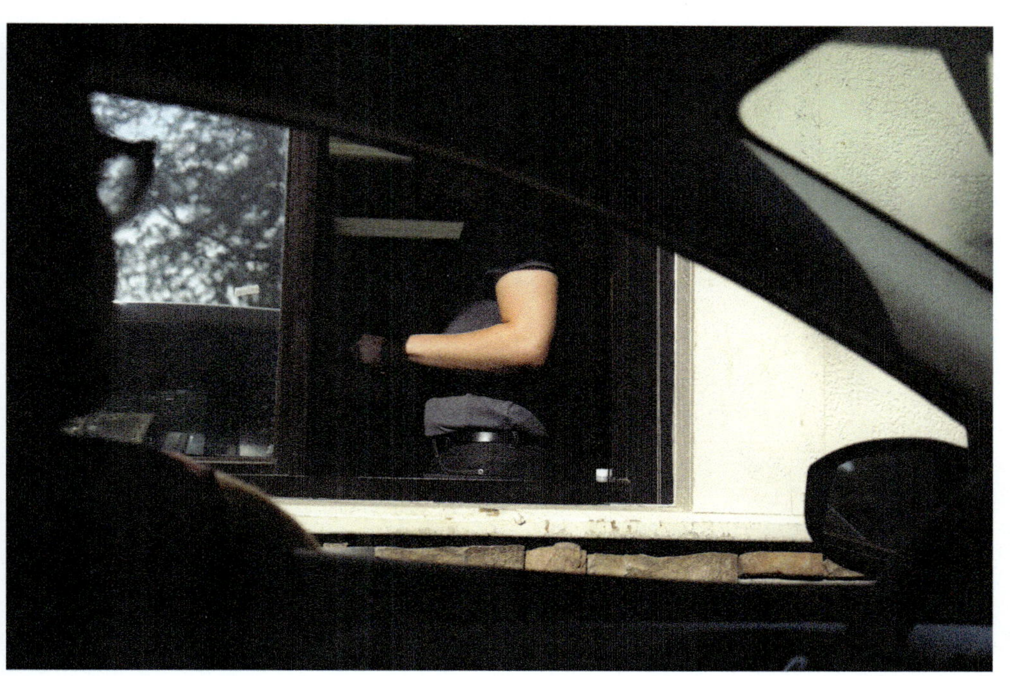

Drive-Thru, Lawrence, KS, 2018

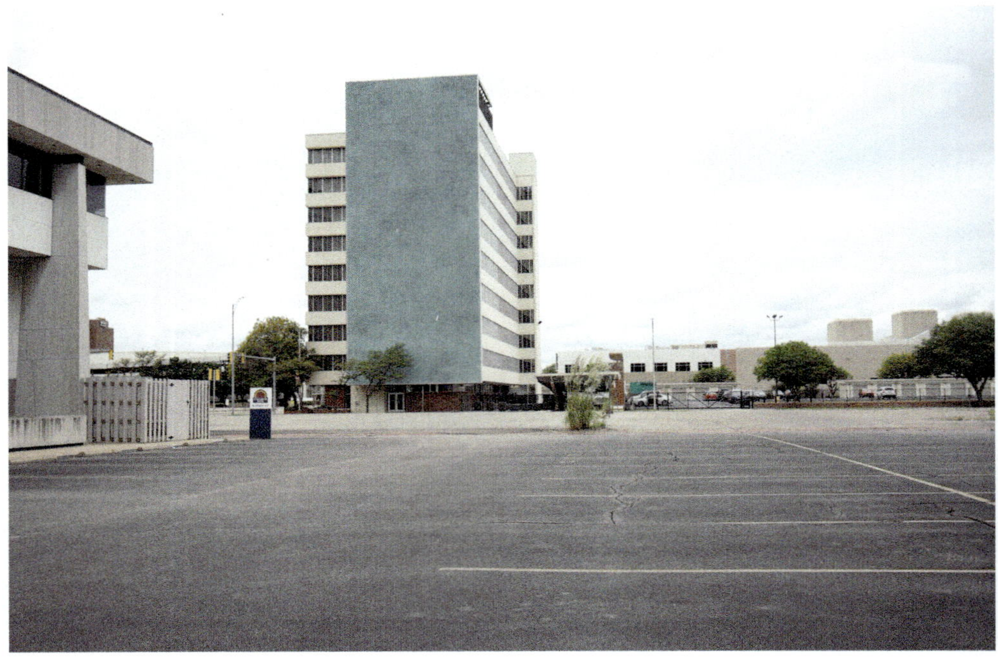

Wichita, KS (former site of the first White Castle), 2018

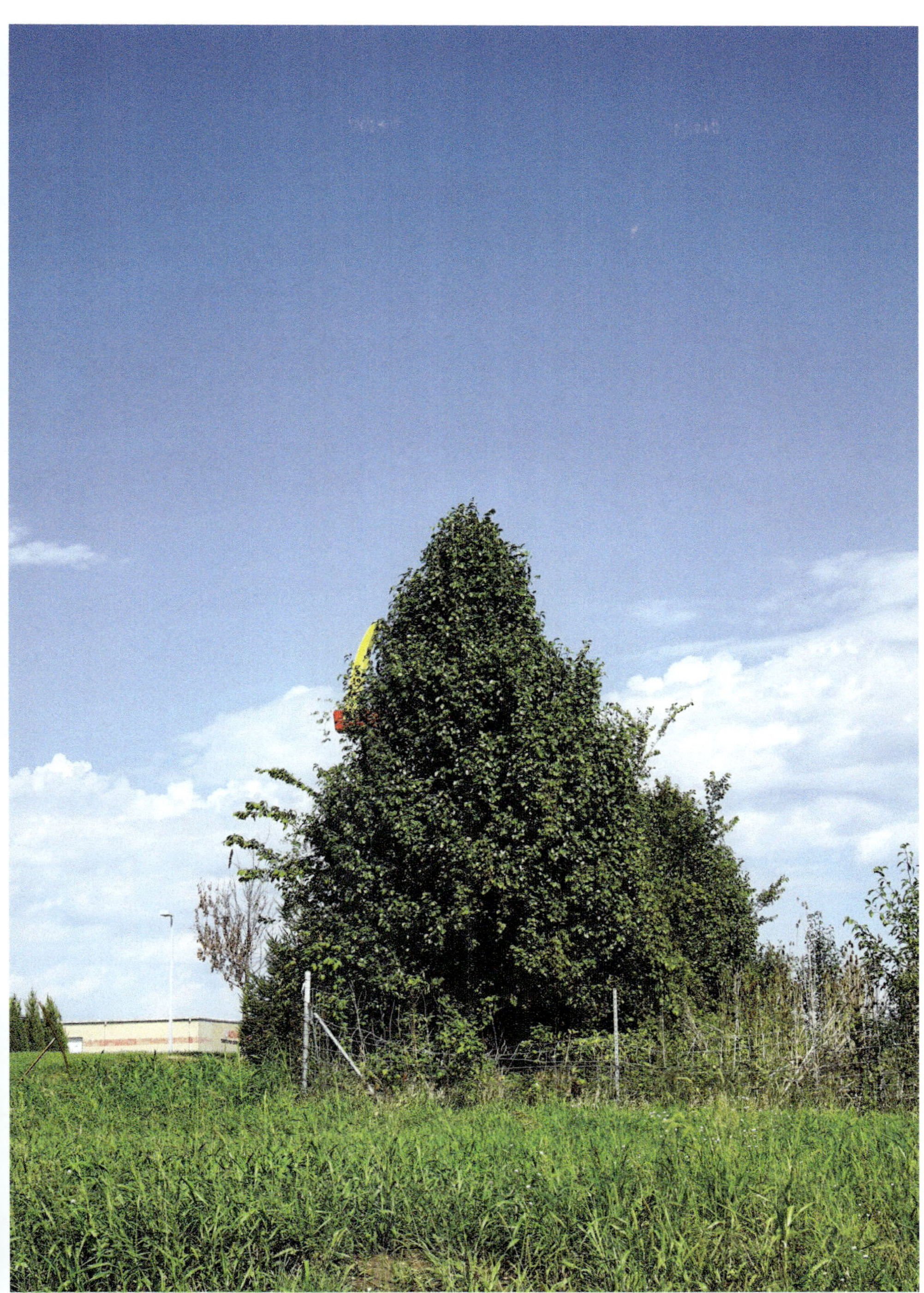

Obscured Restaurant Sign, De Soto, KS, 2018

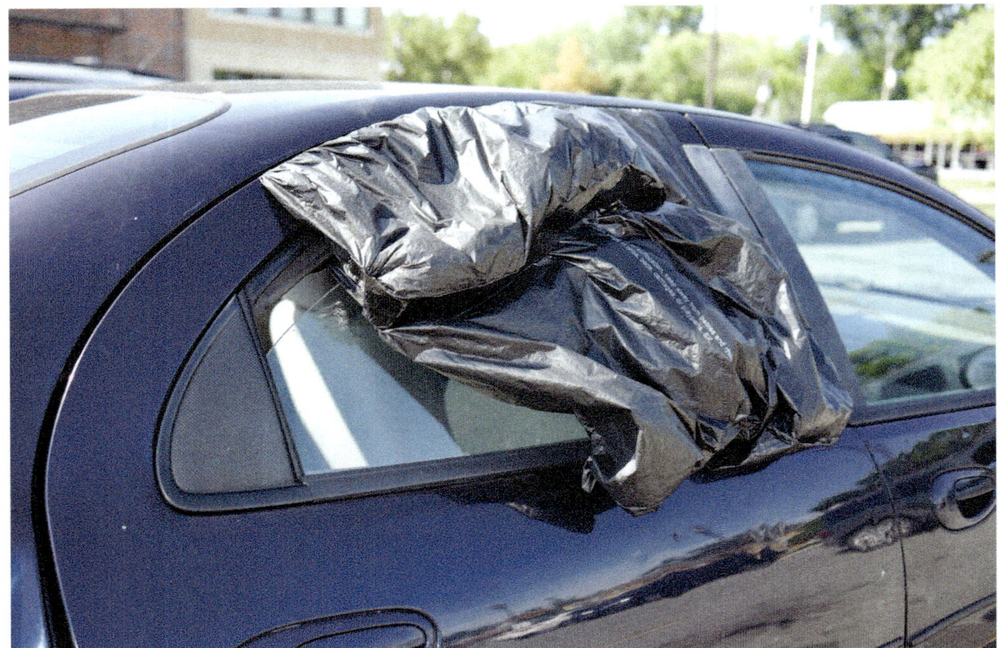

Wrapped Window in Parking Lot, Lawrence, KS, 2018

Chicago Dog #2, Wichita, KS, 2018

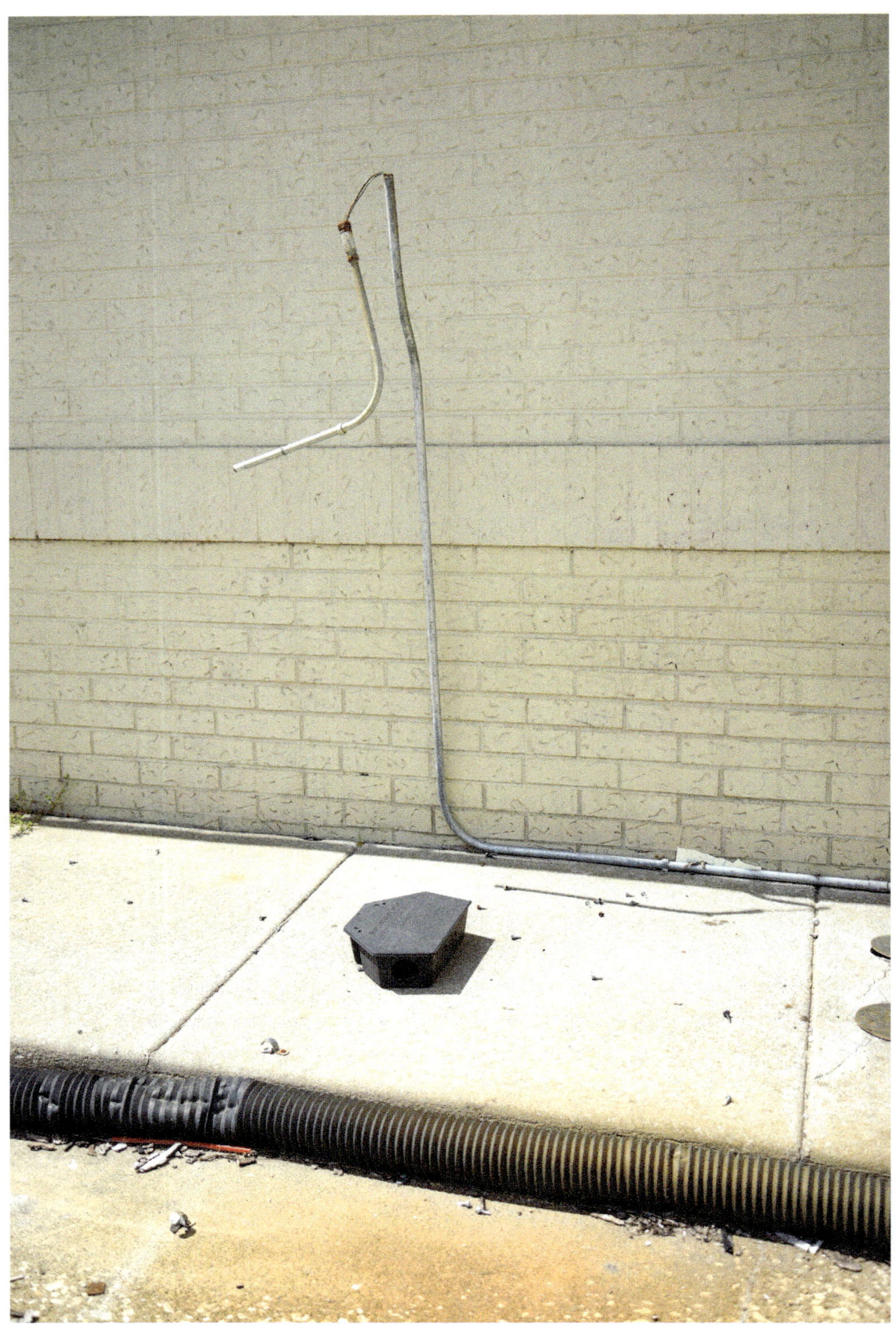

"Kansas Buffet Company" Rat Trap, Topeka, KS, 2018

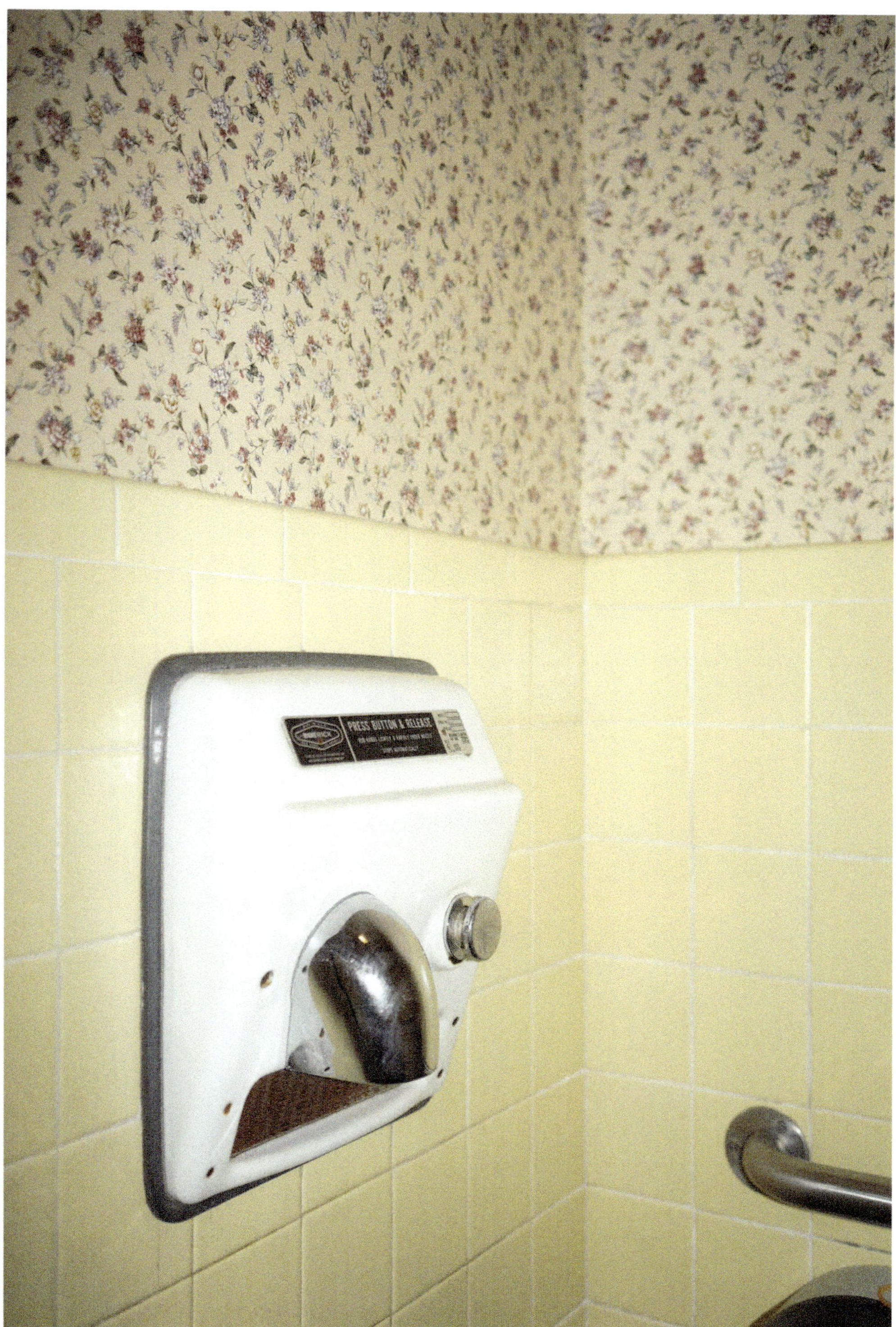

Hand Dryer, Manhattan, KS, 2018

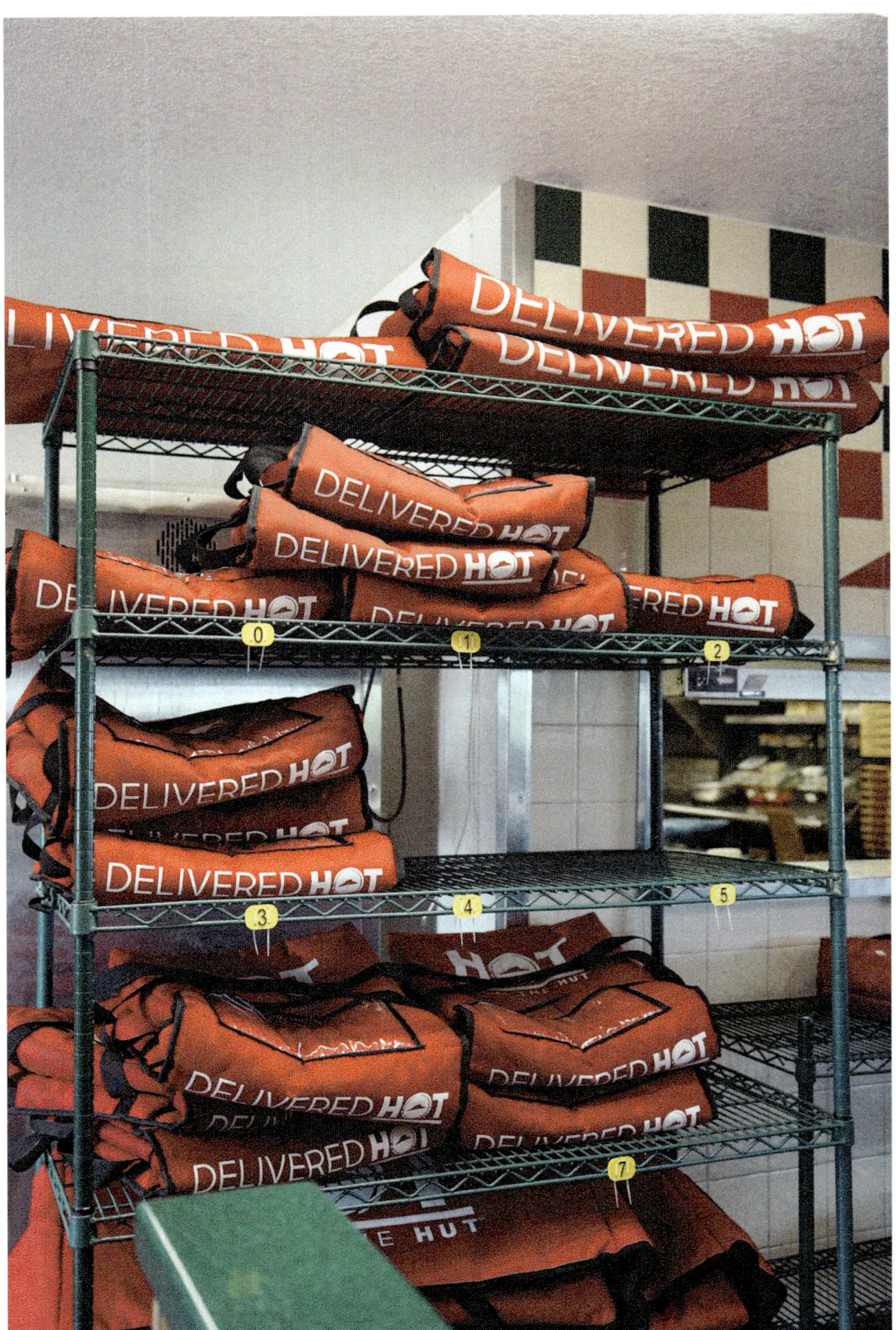

Delivery Bags, De Soto, KS, 2018

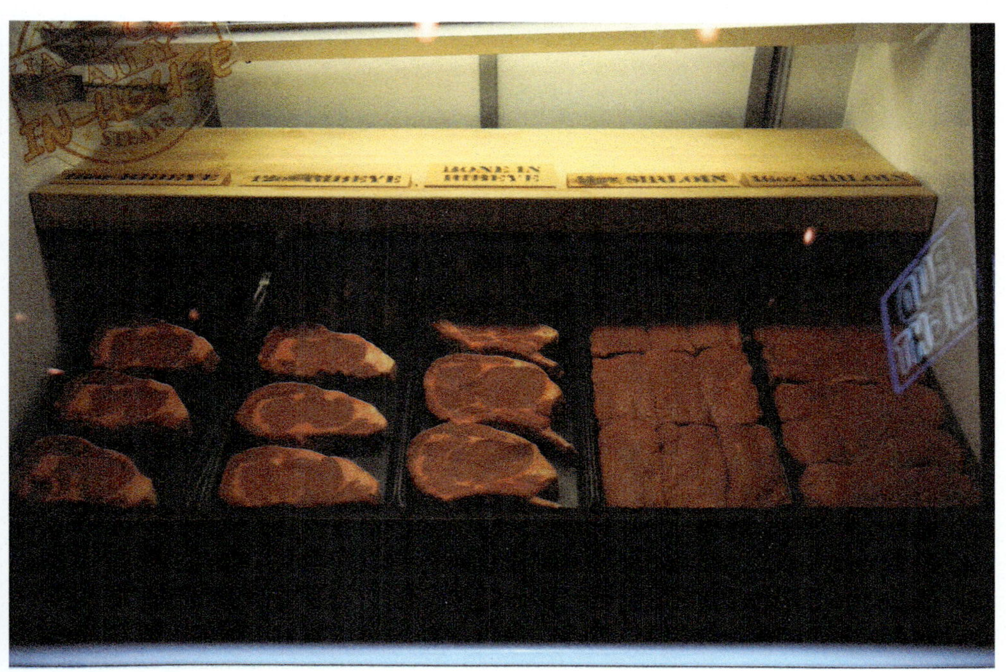

Meat, Lawrence, KS, 2018

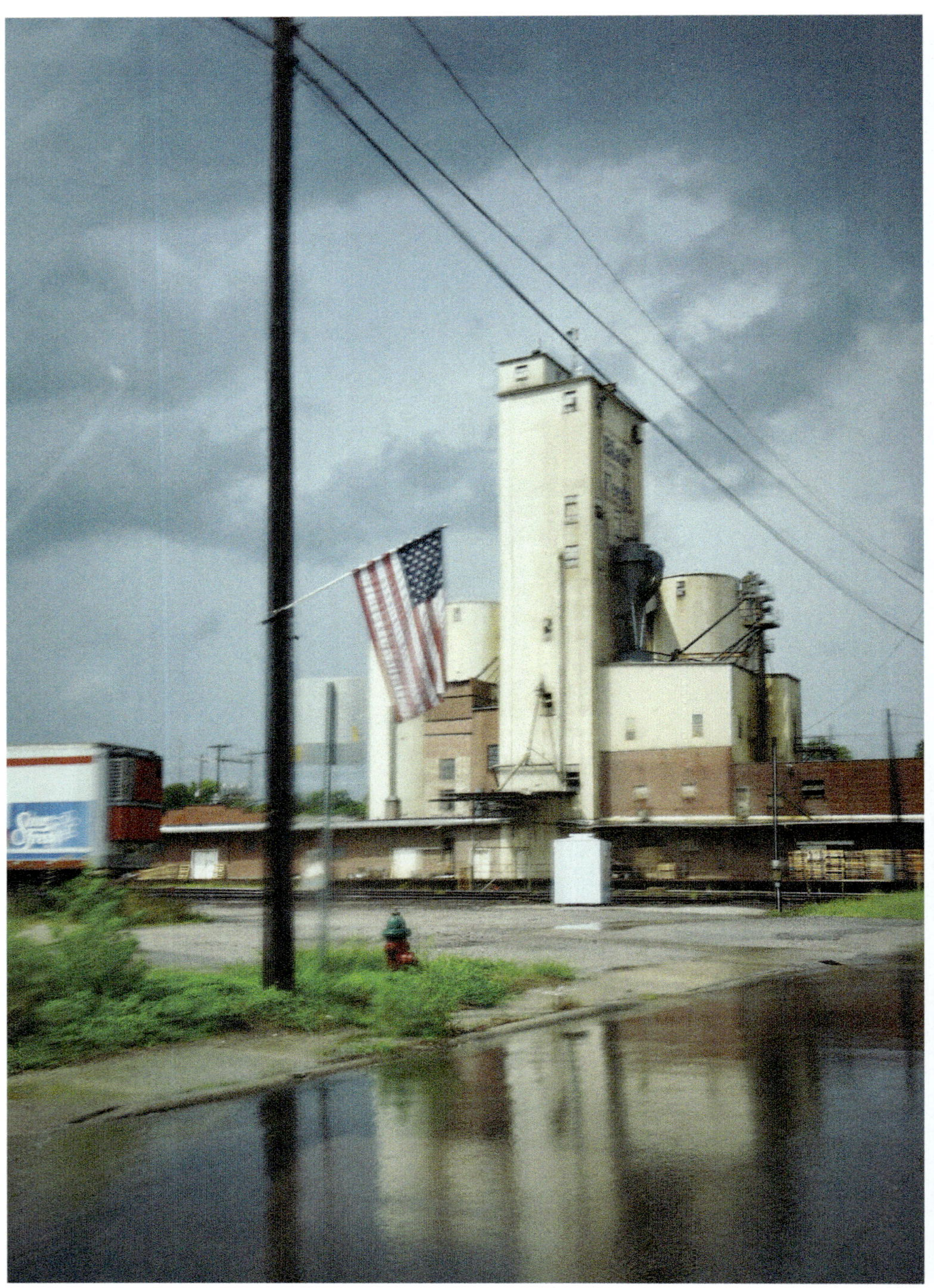

Near Taco John's, Atchison, KS, 2018

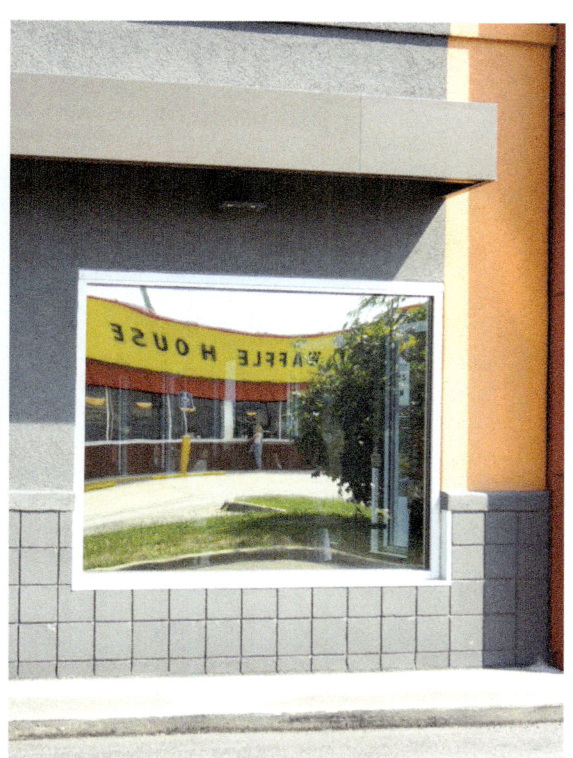

Waffle House Reflection in Window of KFC, Bonner Springs, KS, 2018

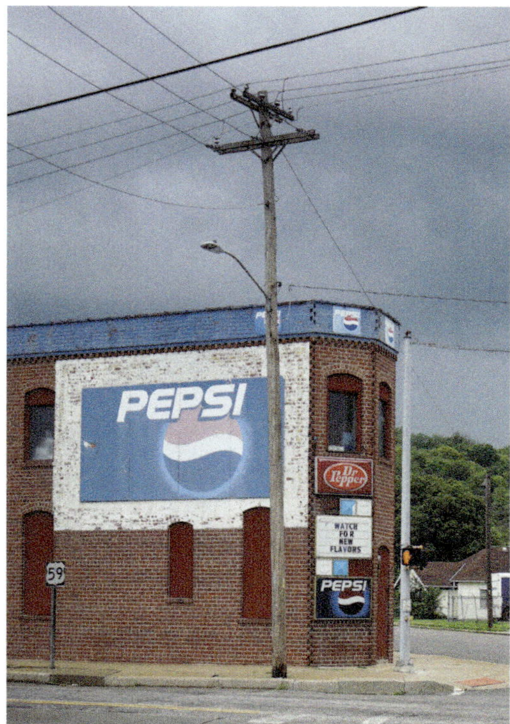

Pepsi, St. Joseph, MO, 2018

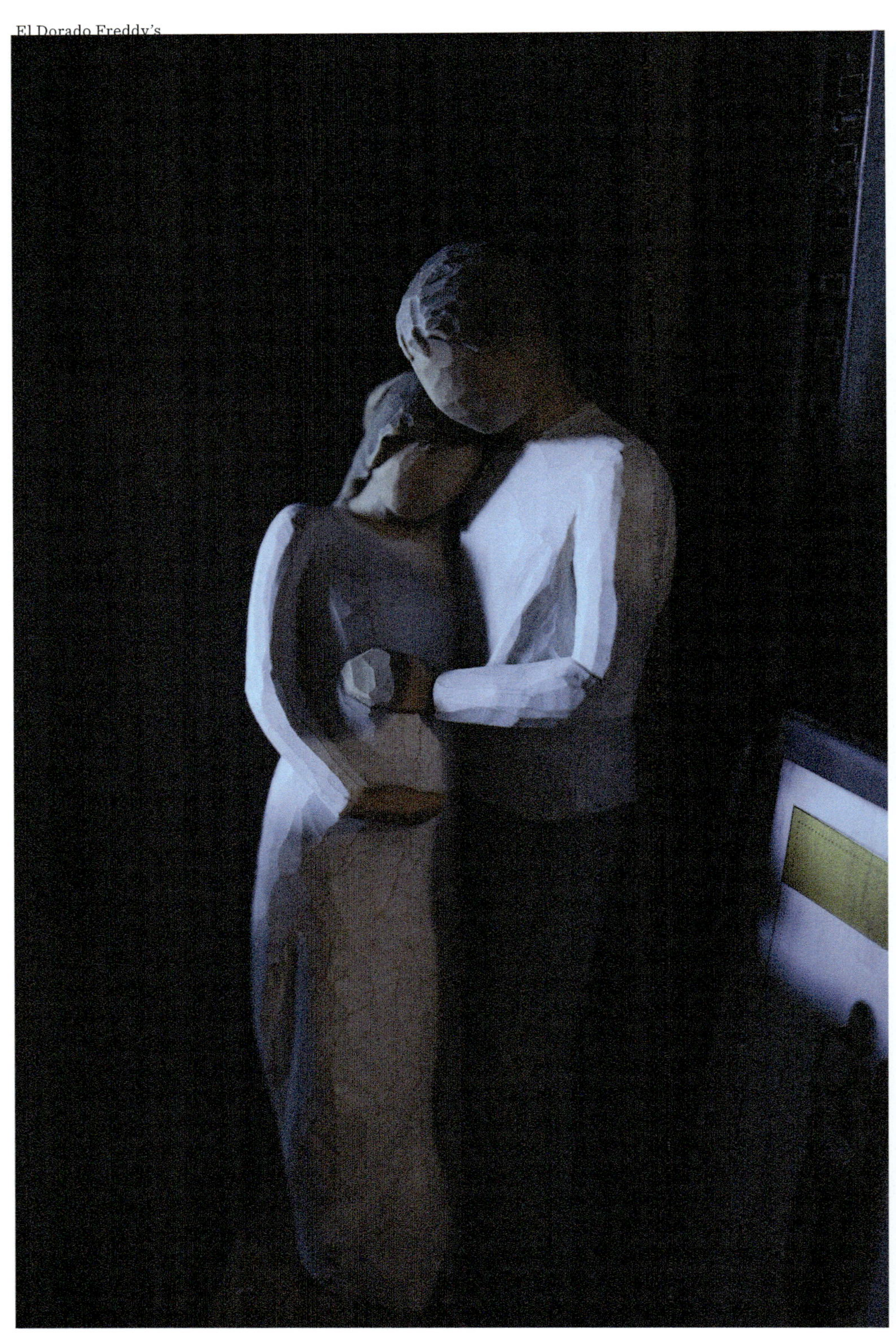

Willow Tree ® "Home" Figurine for Sale at Cracker Barrel, Topeka, KS, 2018

PANERA

"Millennial consumers are more attracted than their elders to cooking at home, ordering delivery from restaurants and eating quickly, in fast-casual or quick-serve restaurants,"

—Buffalo Wild Wings CEO Sally Smith, quoted in the *Business Insider* article, "Millennials are killing chains like Buffalo Wild Wings and Applebee's"

Look at all these millennials!
This place is swarming with us—
it's like the Starbucks
of chain restaurants. There are
millenials on their phones.
Millennials playing Pokemon Go.
Millennials by the fireplace.
There's even a Millennial right here
writing a poem! I love all of it.
Give me a thingy to flash n' buzz
when my sandwich is ready.
Put a really cool word in the title
of that sandwich: Bacon Turkey
Bravo! Give me comfort
in knowing that no matter what
I eat here, it's healthy because
this is Panera! BBQ Chicken
Mac n Cheese with 1180 calories?
This is Panera so they're good
calories! Put some lemon slices
in a bucket next to the iced tea.
Let me ask for water and fill
the tiny cup with Diet Pepsi
when nobody's looking. Let me
memorize every Panera on I-70

and which mile marker to order from
so the food will be ready when I roll up.
Panera, why won't you bring back
baked chips? It's okay, we accept you
for who you are because you
accept us for who we are:
Our yoga pants. Our toy drones.
Our gig economy. Our entitlement.
Our refusal to invest in real estate.
Panera you have an app. Panera
you know when my birthday is
and you give me 99-cent pastries
all month. Panera you're our sword.
We hoist you to behead Applebee's
Cheescake Factory, and B-Dubs too.

Address: Panera Bread Café #368, 528 W. 23rd St., Lawrence, KS 66046
Eaten: Bacon Turkey Bravo sandwich with chips, a water cup filled with Diet Pepsi ($9.26)
With: Poet, alone
Why: Any time I need a healthy meal on the go, it's hard to argue with Panera! It's like a meal delivery kit, but it's a building!

FIRST WATCH

I'm ashamed to even say this:
I downloaded an app
so we could get a spot in line
before we even got here.

Now that I'm a father,
some compromises are worth it—
the First Watch corporation knows
my location at all times, but

at least the time between car and table
is now short enough to nurse
this nap. The food, like it is
at any brunch place,

isn't that big of a fucking deal.
I don't like to make generational
generalizations, but we
millennials sure do love

to wait in line for hours
to eat overpriced eggs.
Today, though, we're seated app-fast
and they have those cradle things

for the car seat and enough room
to put it at the end of our table
without an errant waiter knocking
you over. The server even compliments

your eyes. It might not be worth
an hour on the sidewalk by the nail place,
but eggs are eggs, and the places
downtown don't have cradle things.

Address: First Watch, 2540 Iowa St., Lawrence, KS 66046
Eaten: Decaf coffee with The Trifecta (scrambled, bacon, blueberry pancake), Cold Brew Coffee with the Tri-Athlete Omlette ($28.42 before tip)
Who: Poet + Kara + the Baby
Why: The plan was to pay the rent, go to the grocery store, and be home for lunch, but a baby can really muck up that kind of plan and after paying rent we were starving. Kara wanted eggs. She was the driver.

CHILI'S

"Along the way, I encounter what I consider to be the real enemy, the thing to be feared, marginalized, and kept at a distance at all costs. If ever there was a vision of evil, look at [...] millions of them spreading all across America like herpes."
—Anthony Bourdain, on Chili's

My whole life I've been jealous
when other tables get plates that sizzle
but look at me now, with a margarita
in a little pitcher thing, shaken

25 times on the way to the table. They even
left the pitcher thing here with a little extra. Why
we went out in the middle of your growth spurt
is a product of fatigue, as is my order—

a plate of very salty things
making me notice small cuts in my mouth
I didn't know I had. It makes me confused
about whether I'm hungry or not, like a baby

in a growth spurt. Kara drops
a piece of lettuce onto your ear.
You don't notice; she soon gives up
on the salad. She says it's unrelated.

None of our food sizzles at any point.
I'm not even sure what to order
to get something that sizzles. Perhaps
the Quesadilla Explosion Salad?

Tony said he'd take a crowbar to Chili's.
I'd help. I'm forced to pay on something
called a zee-osk, which is filthy
and makes me take a survey.

In the comments section,
it's all I can do not to write
"I don't think I'll bring my baby back
to this restaurant any more."

Address: Chilis, 2319 Iowa St., Lawrence, KS 66049
Eaten: 1 Presidente Margarita, 1 Grilled Chicken Salad, 1 Smokehouse combo (chicken & sausage) ($46.38. Seems like a lot, right?)
Who: Poet + Kara + the Baby
Why: Oh man, we just had to get out of the house. Someone said Chili's, someone else agreed.

WAFFLE HOUSE

"It is, indeed, marvelous. An irony-free zone where everything is beautiful and nothing hurts. Where everybody, regardless of race, creed, color, or degree of inebriation, is welcomed. Its warm yellow glow a beacon of hope and salvation [...] A place of safety and nourishment."
—Anthony Bourdain, on Waffle House

1.

Last year, Christmas morning, month 4, showing—
Kara fell in the parking lot between the hotel
and the Waffle House. It wasn't our last hour
begging the internet to tell us you'd be okay,
but it was the worst. By the time we emerged
from the greasy air, hashbrown bloated and
walking into fogs of our own breath, we
were pretty sure everything would be okay.

2.

Every few weeks Kara and I hear gunshots
from the bedroom, but we tell ourselves
they're fireworks. We wake up but you don't.
Last summer Kansas passed a law
allowing guns on college campuses. I fear
for Kara who still has to go on campus, and
I fear for whatever guns and schools will
look like when your time comes. A month
before you were born, a shooting
at a Waffle House left four people dead.
You were almost here and I wondered
if anywhere would be safe for you.

3.

The Waffle House Index is a measure
of a storm's power: Red means no power,
no food, go somewhere else and fast.
I keep trying to say the year you were born
was a storm, this one *inside* the Waffle House too.
But these red booths, these white globe lights,
these nicknamed hashbrown options erase
everything on the other side of the big windows.
Maybe the storm's inside some Waffle Houses,
but not this one. We come here every Thanksgiving
and sometimes Christmas too. We recognize people.

4.

Now you're here and Tony's gone.
I guess the storm was inside him too.
He died when you were very young and very bad
at sleeping. It made sense to watch his show
all night bouncing you on the yoga ball. I hope
you have his curiosity. You already have his love
for Waffle House: you won't stop mugging
at the waitresses long enough for us to take
a picture. A waitress gives you a hat. Leaving,
I say I'm full of joy. Kara says she's full of waffle.

Address: 1405 N. Cassady Ave., Columbus, OH 43219
Eaten: Always the same thing: Kara gets a Waffle, scrambled eggs, and bacon, plus a lecture about the fact that Waffle House doesn't really do a la carte ordering. I get the two egg breakfast, over easy, with hashbrowns smothered, chunked, and capped. A side of bacon if I'm feeling festive. I was feeling festive.
With: Poet + Kara + the Baby
Why: Thanksgiving and Christmas are in Columbus because your great grandma lives there. The cheapest hotel by her place doesn't have free breakfast, but the Waffle House is right across the parking lot.

CHIK-FIL-A

Son, imagine a place where they hand out nuggets for free
on the end of toothpicks. Special nuggets called Bourbon Chicken.
This magical place was named Food Court It lived inside
a "Mall" which was basically a parking garage for stores.
Malls used to be everywhere. They're gone now, mostly replaced
by Amazon warehouses. When I was a kid, we'd go to the mall
when we couldn't figure out what else to do. The best place
to get nuggets at a Food Court was Chik-fil-A. Our family doesn't
agree with how the Chik-fil-A corporation blends its business with its
fundamentalist values. Everything is political, even malls:
they leveled neighborhoods and killed the idea of a downtown.
Even Amazon: they killed the idea of buying things from people
in a building. That used to be possible! We'd drive a car ourselves
to a building and give money to a person in exchange for food
or other stuff. Everything is political, even nuggets. But Chik-fil-A's
nuggets are brined in pickle juice before being fried and are therefore
irresistible. I understand. Still, before you ask your Alexa implant
to send a Chik-fil-A drone, think about the cost, the real cost,
of those chicken nuggets.

Address: Chik-fil-A inside the Westridge Mall, 1801 SW Wanamaker Rd., Topeka, KS 66604: NOW CLOSED
Eaten: 8 piece nuggets (they gave me 12!) and a Diet Coke ($6.20)
With: Poet + the Baby
Why: Kara had an Old Navy gift card to spend, so the poet and the baby, like a good Midwestern family, go for a walk in a mall that is dying but not yet dead.

THREE SMALL POEMS ABOUT THREE SMALL CHAINS

1.

NuWay's most controversial belief is
that "crumbly is better," that a hamburger
should be loose and taste like stale cooking grease.
Not great, but certainly no cause for boycott.

2.

Dog-N-Shake believes "everything"
means onions, a mixture of relish
and mustard, and celery salt. Find me
in the streets, marching for that.

3.

Vista isn't even a chain anymore, it's a link
to the neon past, especially T's, especially this limeade.
The past is never as good as you remember. Lunch
is never just lunch but here it comes close.

Address: 1. NuWay, 1416 W Douglas Ave., Wichita, KS 67203
2. Dog-N-Shake, 4323 S. Seneca, Wichita, KS 67214
3. Vista Drive-In, 1911 Tuttle Creek Blvd., Manhattan, KS 66502

Eaten: 1. One Medium Nu-Way and a Root Beer ($3.29)
2. One hot dog with everything and a limeade ($5.46)
3. One Vistaburger with a limeade ($5.68)

With: Poet & T

Why: We went in search of photos, we went in search of the past, we went in search of cheap food we could eat in good conscience. We found limeade.

CHICKEN FINGER

I cannot find the origin for the term "chicken finger," though there are indications it predates the term "chicken tender" *see also* a restaurant in Savannah, Spanky's, claims to have invented the Chicken Finger in 1976 *see also* The first restaurant to pop up when you Google "Chicken Finger" is Raising Cane's *see also* though my middle name is Adam, and I now have a son who shares my last name, "Adam Raised A Cain" is not my favorite Bruce Springsteen song *see also* Raising Cane's is not my favorite place to get chicken fingers *see also* as I raise this Caine I wonder if he'll be picky too *see also* I want him to have fun eating *see also* I want him to have fun eating something other than *the pectoralis minor muscle, commonly coated in a breading mixture and deep fried in a manner similar to the preparation of schnitzel*

FREDDY'S

You're sleeping. We don't touch anything,
don't change the air don't change speeds
holy shit we might actually make it
to Wichita on time. My phone tells me
that it's the birthplace of fast food
but I don't want to say it out loud
because it might startle you awake.
White Castle was first, Freddy's followed
nearly a century later but it's possible
to eat at Freddy's without self-hatred
and a forever smelly car. White Castle
took down its Wichita towers
a half century ago, but Freddy's
loves its hometown enough to erect
a billboard on the outskirts declaring
how much. Out of fear things might
explode before Wichita we stop
in El Dorado where everything sounds
magical: El Dorado Dollar Tree. El Dorado
Wine & Spirits. El Dorado *Freddy's.*
The steakburgers are perfect.
Mustard pickle onion cheese.
Freddy's knows not to fuck with
tomatoes. Salt, crunch, wolf
it down in the front seat praying
you stay asleep. Jesus Christ
this jalapeno fry sauce is liquid
gold. I want to eat it like soup
with little fry croutons. I want
to declare that Freddy's should be
more famous but I'm afraid to make
noise beyond happy burger sounds.

Switch drivers. Insert Tom Petty's
greatest hits and say a prayer
you stay happy. Oh yeah, all right,
take it easy baby make it last all night,
or at least the next thirty three miles.

Address: Freddy's Frozen Custard & Steakburgers, 1809 W. Central, El Dorado, KS 67402
Eaten: Two original double combos, one root beer, one Diet Dr. Pepper. Lots and lots of jalapeno fry sauce.
With: Poet + Kara + the Baby
Why: The baby started to seem like maybe he was waking up, even though we were only a half hour out of Wichita. We ate in the parking lot. He didn't wake up at all.

SPANGLES

We drink relief like Diet Coke:
you made it to Wichita
without turning tornado.
I leave you with Kara at the hotel
and drive to this sockhop dream—
don't call it kitsch, call it
make America neon again.
Elvis again. Marilyn again.
This star spangled past
never existed but now it does,
at Broadway and Dewey,
until 10 pm. It's an accident
but I order an Oriental
Chicken Salad and
a Gyro. Though it's delicious,
tonight my homeland is nothing
but a hotel room: You, Kara,
House Hunters on a cheap flatscreen,
and a salad spilled all over my shirt.

Address: Spangles, 612 S. Broadway, Wichita KS 67202
Eaten: Original Gyro, Oriental Chicken Salad ($12.34)
With: Poet, bringing food back to the hotel for his family
Why: Dinner ended up being rushed (it's hard to get a baby anywhere on a schedule) and immediately upon returning to the hotel after the reading, I realized with horror that I hadn't eaten a single vegetable all day.

RED LOBSTER

"And to visit there is rather special"
—Marilyn Hagerty

I've got nothing: this place
is fine. There are a lot of people
here, and they're all having
a good time. The biscuits are,
in fact, delicious. Sure,
every table has a tiny binder
full of cocktails and cakes.
But I still had fun and ate
a pretty good plate of food.

———

Address: Red Lobster, 2011 SW Wanamaker Rd., Topeka, KS 66604
Eaten: Create your own shellfish combo with Shrimp Scampi and Sea Scallops, Crab-Topped Tilapia, Key Lime Pie to share, and just a shit ton of Cheddar Bay Biscuts ($52.66)
With: Poet + Kara + the Baby
Why: Kara: "You've never been to *Red Lobster*?"

ARBY'S

  Never get anything other than the thing,
especially here. Beef
  really should be what's
for dinner, or in this case,
  breastfeeding lunch. This
is what these places don't
  understand: Nobody wants
plain fries here
  or this godawful chicken
sandwich crumbling
  into my lap and corners I didn't
know the Prius had. We don't go
  here for interior design ideas.
We go to feel Western
  if Western means hard
white plastic chairs and Horsey Sauce
  squirted into a paper cup.
I don't have a TV, and I don't want
  to order lunch from one.
I want to stop
  just long enough for you
to get fed and for me to enter
  a space that serves the same food
and looks the same way
  it did when I was your age.

Address: Arby's, 2711 W. US Highway 50, Emporia, KS 66801
Eaten: 1 Regular Roast Beef Combo (Curly Fries, A&W), 1 Pecan Chicken Salad Sandwich Combo (Curly Fries, Diet Dr. Pepper)
With: Poet + Kara + the Baby
Why: Kara loves little more than a Roast Beef and Cheese Sticks, but the baby might have a dairy insensitivity? Maybe he's just fussy. The first weeks of the first child have been a flurry of shifting worries. Anyway, the rule goes, she who feeds the baby picks the restaurant.

TACO JOHN'S

Look at this, I tell Kara.
Every picture Laura posts of her baby
is happy. "She's the love of my life,
I love to hear her talking." *Talking?*
She's the same age as our kid.
Our kid's not talking. What if
Laura has a smarter baby? Kara
chews, then says *I don't*
think this is a healthy
line of questioning. I chew.
There's nothing quite like
a Potato Olé. Don't tell me
they're just hashbrowns.
Fine, I say. *There's always this:*
even if her baby is smarter, at least
we have Taco John's here.

Address: Taco John's, 1101 W 6th St., Lawrence KS 66044
Eaten: A bigass thing of potato olés and tons of hot sauce ($2.39)
With: Poet + Kara
Why: It's a law of the universe: as soon as the words "Potato Olé" are spoken out loud, you must acquire some lest the craving become too overwhelming.

CICI'S PIZZA

This restaurant is as sad
as you are. On the wall,
a huge monochromatic child
eats a hunk of something.
The photo is labeled with
one unpunctuated word: fun.
None of this is. In college
we used to pack the whole
house into cars for Cici's night.
The thing about nostalgia is
maybe it doesn't work
if the thing wasn't fun
to begin with. Kara and I
take turns bouncing you
and eating various crimes
against pizza. Finally
you fall asleep on my shoulder.
I can't see your face but Kara
says you looks sweet, like a
slice of powdered sugar brownie.
In the mirror in the back
of the game room claw machine,
I see you. You do.

Address: Cici's Pizza, 2020 W. 23rd St., Suite A, Lawrence, KS 66046: NOW CLOSED
Eaten: Two buffets, two drinks, sixteen bucks
With: Poet + Kara + the Baby
Why: I don't care how easily Cici's fits into the route of your errands, or how family-friendly it seems, or how cheap, or how much it reminds you of a good time in your life. It's not worth it.

SIMPLE SIMON'S

This was not the right day to visit St. Joseph.
It won't stop raining and the whole place smells.
T is picking up bad vibes. I've heard
there's a Simple Simon's here and I'm interested
in taste as time travel. I won't get into particulars
but a Simple Simon's was important
to me for a few summers long ago. Plan:
drive to St. Joe, eat a calzone, and go back
to those summers. Except the calzone tastes
different. Too yeasty. T and I argue about whether
the bug she saw was a cockroach. On top of it all
a baby starts crying and he sounds exactly like you.
T asks if this is the farthest from you I've ever been.
She's seen it on my face: it is.

Address: Simple Simon's Pizza, 5123 Lake Ave., St Joseph, MO 64504
Eaten: One calzone, one fountain drink ($12)
With: Poet + T
Why: "Simple Simon…now that's a name I've not heard in a long time."

RUNZA

On a dad-solo shopping trip, I decide
to finally figure out what the hell a Runza is.
It's ground beef with some other stuff baked
into bread. A Nebraska thing, apparently.
It's greasy good. Without thinking, I order
the one that shares your name.

Address: Runza, 27th & Iowa St., Lawrence, KS 66046
With: Poet, alone
Eaten: 1 Spicy Jack Runza ($5.77)
Why: Look, I'm not saying I'm dying to get away from the baby or anything. I've always been annoyed by narratives of parenting that just go nuts on how awful it is. If I were to dwell on only the awful things for long enough to write a poem about them, I'm sure I'd lose all grip. Sleeplessness gets worse when you think about sleeplessness. So since the beginning, I've tried to at least tell people that if not fun, having a baby is less hard than I expected. A narrative of having my shit together would perhaps help me have my shit together. Maybe it's hubris. That said, I do appreciate the chance to have an hour alone. Even if it's at Target. I planned on buying a $25 box of diapers and I walked out with $90 in stuff. Part of that is because, even though I'm having this empowering quiet alone moment, I keep seeing things that Kara would like. When I get to the car, the song that comes on the radio is "Naïve Melody (This Must Be The Place)," which happens to be my favorite song in part because it captures the perfect ambivalence of being in a family. Of course, it brings to mind you and Kara. I start the car and point it towards the apartment, in a hurry to get back to you. To hold either or both of you. But not before I grab a quick bite. We're getting a babysitter for the first time tonight. It's just Kara's mom, and Kara insists it'll only be for an hour. We're gonna grab dinner. Of course we're going to go a nice place. A restaurant that only has one location. Every time I go there, I see someone I know.

PIZZA HUT: OUR STORY

In 1958, two brothers borrowed $600 from their mom to open a pizza place in Wichita, Kansas.

In 2018, your parents took you to Pizza Hut.

We have more than 16,000 restaurants and 350,000 team members in more than 100 countries.

A poem about Pizza Hut must sprawl like suburbs,
from crust to shining crust.

There's nothing cookie-cutter about Pizza Hut.

They don't make Kansas Pizza Huts like Ohio Pizza Huts. An Ohio Pizza Hut is a magic place. Lunch buffet. A stained glass lamp over every table. Curtains. Down and to the side, there's a little smoked glass room that used to be the smoking section but now it's just "the Garden Room." In Kansas, a Pizza Hut can look like anything. Many don't even have that red roof. Many are in strip malls. The one in Lawrence is yellow and looks like a Taco Bell.

Wichita, Kansas

invented it but I guess it's been perfected elsewhere. Let me peek
between trees to see a scarlet roof, pause in the door's hot pizza breath
while my eyes adjust to burgundy darkness. Pizza Hut
should be for paydays and kids who've filled Book It cards.

Pizza Hut was built on the belief that pizza night should be special

when we're moving
when our son is born
at a high school lock in
trying to get people to a meeting
every Friday in the cafeteria
when we're celebrating
when the mailbox coupons are good
during the Super Bowl
every time we go to Columbus
when we miss being a kid
when we both worked until 5 and there are no groceries
until we can't anymore
order three, so my brother and I can both have dinner and
the next two lunches
when the party is winding down
when the party is winding up
when we don't want to put pants on to go get nuggets
when we can't think of anything else
when we learn the baby doesn't actually have a dairy insensitivity

The service felt like home. And the customers were treated like family.

We're trying so hard to have fun. The manager, who takes breaks from something apparently urgent to wait on us, is acting like she's never seen dine-in customers. At the end of every interaction she sprints to the kitchen. Someone leans behind the counter looking at her phone. It is unclear whether she works here. The pizza tastes like a good impression of Pizza Hut pizza.

the ingredients we use are still our highest priority.

It's gotta be the cheese. No other cheese on earth tastes like this. It has a reputation for being greasy, but what pizza doesn't leave a ghost of itself on the empty box?

the belief that pizza night

always sounds better in advance

They named it Pizza Hut, because their sign only had room for eight letters.

PIZZA SAD
PIZZA WHY
GAS PAINS
PIZZA ASS
SO GREASY
NOPE NOPE
A BAD IDEA
SETTLING

We don't just make pizza. We make people happy.

Kara frowns and looks around. She says
"I could do cartwheels in here."

Address: 600 W. 23rd St., Lawrence, KS 66046
Eaten: Large pizza, half pepperoni half mushroom, an order of breadsticks, a Diet Coke, a Root Beer, neighborhood of 26 bucks.
With: Poet + Kara + the Baby
Why: Kara wanted to welcome cheese back into her life with a joyful experience, but the Pizza Huts are actually better in different states: namely, Ohio and the Past.

HU HOT MONGOLIAN BARBEQUE

with a nod to "Jewish Enough" by Emily Sernaker

Well, we took you to your first vigil today.
Two days ago a man barged into a bris
in Pittsburgh and murdered eleven people.

As he killed them, he shouted *all Jews must die.*
We don't know how Jewish you're going to be,
but I'm Jewish so that makes you Jewish

enough. May this be your last vigil.
My most Jewish instinct is this: when
I feel sad and Jewish, I get hungry.

Our people's languages are Hebrew, Yiddish,
and food. How perfect is this place, then.
We can eat as much as we want and the food

never runs out. The choices multiply like
grains of sand. Even the pop menu (the pop menu!)
has two hundred options. Some would rob us

of the choice to live, or the choice to live
a day in this country without having to mourn
a mass shooting. Here, though, we confront

infinity only through combinations of grill items
and soda flavors. None of these choices
has consequences. Next time I can pick

cherry lime Diet Dr. Pepper instead of Grape Fanta—
Burn-Your-Village Barbeque sauce instead of
Feed-the-Hordes Hoisin—and nothing will happen.

Here I can choose to hoist you above my head
and sing along to background Blues Traveler while
you and your mom fill the empty room with laughs

a half hour after we sang *Oseh Shalom*
on the patio in front of the union
with a few dozen others. Both songs

need singing. Which one I sing and when
should be a choice, like which six scoops of sauce
I ladle into my bowl. I choose. I choose.

Where: 2525 Iowa St., Lawrence, KS 66046
Eaten: Two Create Your Own Grill Meals at the dinner price, plus a hot & sour soup and an egg drop soup and a bowl of rice, a cherry lime Diet Dr. Pepper, and a Grape Fanta ($40 after tip)
With: Poet + Kara + the Baby
Why: The vigil was on campus and the parking garage spit us out headed down Iowa towards the chains. I was determined to carve out some kind of joy today. We passed lots of restaurants: Raisin Canes, not joyful. Pie Five Pizza, not joyful. B-Dubs, definitely not joyful. Hu Hot: this seemed like a place where we could find joy.

BURGER KING

You know the elevator song
and rib nibbles and the difference
between jumper, bouncer, rocker,
and sleeper. You know Sophie
and Boppy and Taggies and Moby
and Zipadeezip and Wubanub
and Bumbo but you know nothing
of days packed so tight
the only option for lunch
is whichever drive thru has no line
because you're just a baby
watching me eat chicken nuggets
while we wait for Kate to get here
so I can go back to work, another
thing you don't know anything about.
Tomorrow I won't remember
what the hell even made this morning
so busy but I will remember the strange
delight you find in watching me
chew, that all it takes to make you
laugh is taking a bite. They say
it's a sign you'll start food soon,
but you've tried applesauce and
pudding and pickles and you've hated
all of it. You're staring at me.
I extend a hand towards you,
nugget outreached. You part your lips
and taste the nugget and taste it
again. You look at me and smile.

Where: 1107 W 6th St., Lawrence, KS 66044
Who: Poet + the Baby
What: 10 nuggets, a Junior Whopper, and a Diet Coke ($5.49)
Why: Errands + baby = running late always (diaper change in the car trunk, bottle in a parking lot, etc.) and you just can't make a salad when all you have is 10 minutes. Or at least that's what I tell myself.

KRISPY KREME

Son, some advice: you don't know
what a hangover is, but when you learn,
a McDonald's #4 breakfast will help.
Never eat at Subway.
You're allowed to take breadsticks
& salad and/or cheddar bay biscuits
to go. While I'm on the subject
of breadsticks, ask for extra
when you order at Fazoli's
because the basket person might
come around too late or
not at all. Always ask for sauce
at Taco Bell, even if you don't
want it, because they give you
a ton and it's good on tomorrow's
eggs. Finally, if you see
the Krispy Kreme sign
lit up, you must go.
I don't know how to make
magic but I know where
you can go to find it.

Address: Krispy Kreme, 8805 Shawnee Mission Pkwy., Merriam, KS 66202
Eaten: four glazed donuts (5 bucks or so)
With: Poet + Kara + the Baby
Why: The sign was on, duh.

ACKNOWLEDGEMENTS

Danny:

"Popeyes," "Culvers," "In-N-Out Burger," "Cracker Barrel," "Chili's," "Texas Roadhouse," "Wendy's," and "Krispy Kreme" appeared in different form as a serialized column in *Hobart* called *Chain Restaurants Reviewed by Poems.*

Thank you to Aaron Burch for buying into this idea early on and giving the first poems a home.

Thank you to Tara Wray for emailing me out of the blue after reading "Popeye's" and thus beginning a fruitful and rewarding collaboration and friendship.

Thank you to the whole Belt team, including Martha for picking up the book and Anne for running such a great operation.

Thank you to Amanda Teuscher for retweeting Martha's tweet where she said Belt was looking for book ideas.

Thank you to PBR Writer's Club for the endless feedback and a beloved Thursday night ritual: Chance Dibben, Rachel McCarthy James, Richard Noggle, Julia Gilmore Gaughan, Jon Kaleugher, and Brushy.

Thanks the writer-people who have supported me during the writing of this book: Dan Hoyt, Mercedes Lucero, Paige Webb, Phil Metres, Megan Kaminski, Jim McCrary, and Lesley Wheeler.

Thanks to my family for the support, and thanks to Kara and Jack for everything. Jack, these poems are for you.

Tara:

To my family, I offer my greatest thanks. To Danny Caine, for providing the most savory excuse for a trip to Kansas, my home and native land, thank you. To Belt Publishing—Anne Trubek and Martha Bayne—chef's kiss.